LIFE IN COPPER AGE BRITAIN

LIFE IN COPPER AGE BRITAIN

JULIAN HEATH

AMBERLEY

Cover image: Copper axe-heads and dagger from Ballamoar, Isle of Man.
(Manx National Heritage)

First published 2012

Amberley Publishing
The Hill, Stroud
Gloucestershire, GL5 4EP

www.amberleybooks.com

British Library Cataloguing in Publication Data.
A catalogue record for this book is available from the British Library.

ISBN 978 1 84868 790 5

Typeset in 10pt on 12pt Sabon.
Typesetting and Origination by Amberley Publishing.
Printed in the UK.

Contents

Acknowledgements

Many people and organisations have generously supplied images and information for this book. In particular, I would like to thank: Stan Beckensall, Billy O' Brien, David Evans, Alison Sheridan, Simon Timberlake, Mike Parker Pearson, Allison Fox and John Caley at Manx National Heritage, John Hunter, Tim Darvill, Martin Powell, Antony Slegg, Duncan Garrow, Harry Fokkens, Robin Jackson and Victoria Bryant at Worcestershire Historic Environment & Archaeology Service; Peter Hodges, Brian Mutton, Sigurd Towrie, Patrick Clay, Ian Cartwright, Christophe Meneboeuf, Janet Montgomery, Mandy Jay, Jonathon Smith, and Ges Moody at Trust for Thanet Archaeology. I would also like to thank British Museum Images, Ashmolean Museum, Salisbury & South Wiltshire Museum, and Nicola Gale and Tom Furby at Amberley Publishing – sorry about the barrage of images! Finally, I must say a huge thank you to the Author's Foundation who provided me with a very generous grant, which has made the completion of this book an easier task.

INTRODUCTION

As Stuart Needham (2008: 19) has pointed out, although British archaeologists have long been aware that there was a copper-using phase before the advent of the Bronze Age, they have not – until recently – seen fit to define a Copper Age or 'Chacolithic' (after the Greek words for copper and stone) for British prehistory. This unwillingness to add a Copper Age to the long-established three-age system of stone, bronze and iron can probably be explained, at least in part, by the fact that the copper-using phase in Britain was relatively brief, lasting from around 2450–2150 BC (*ibid.*). It is also quite possible that the British Copper Age lasted a little longer than this, as Mike Parker Pearson (2008: 25) believes that the 'balance of probabilities is swinging towards the likelihood of a British Chalcolithic starting at 2600 BC'. This is a view shared by myself, because as we will see in the following pages, there are hints to be found in the archaeological record indicating that Britain's prehistoric communities were using – if not making – copper artefacts as early as the twenty-sixth century BC.

Whatever the true date of the arrival of metalworking on our prehistoric shores, Needham and Parker Pearson sit amongst a number of leading British archaeologists who argue in favour of a Copper Age in Britain rather than a 'Late Neolithic', 'Beaker Period', or 'Early Bronze Age', which are the labels often alternatively given to the latter centuries of the third millennium BC. However, not all archaeologists agree with the idea of a British Copper Age, as was revealed at a major conference on the subject held at Bournemouth University in 2008, with delegates equally divided on whether we are justified in talking of the existence of one in prehistoric Britain (Mullin 2008: 7). I would obviously place myself in the camp of the Copper Age 'advocates', but perhaps we should not be too overly concerned with labels, and with taking sides, as the real importance of this period lies with the evidence that its communities have left behind as a fascinating legacy to their brief lives. This evidence speaks eloquently of a highly dynamic and exciting time of change in prehistoric Britain, and Needham's (2008: 22) comparison of this period to the Renaissance of late medieval Europe is certainly worthy of consideration and should not be rejected as overblown.

This book aims to provide an overview of this evidence and hopefully also offer readers a window onto what is arguably one of the most enthralling periods in British prehistory. Of course, the view through this window can never totally be clear, as thousands of years have passed since the British Copper Age. We are also faced with a massive and somewhat daunting corpus of archaeological evidence dating to this time, and thus it has been necessary to be selective when choosing the material for inclusion in this book, and this in itself has been no easy task. All this writer can do is to apologise to those readers who may be disgruntled by any omissions they feel should have been included, and hope that the narrative in the following chapters goes some way to assuaging their discontentment.

Unsurprisingly, this narrative begins with the growing evidence that it was small groups of immigrants from various parts of the Continent who lie behind the beginning of the Copper Age in Britain. It is also possible that some of these immigrants may have opened up Britain's first copper mines, which will be briefly looked at in Chapter Two; however, as we will see, to find the strongest evidence for this, we actually have to make a diversion to south-western Ireland. As will also be seen, ethnographic insights suggest that we would probably be unwise to view this early copper mining as a functional process that simply consisted of the extraction of raw materials for the production of tools and weapons. Some mention will also be made in this chapter of flint mining, as although the latter is an activity that is often associated with Britain's Neolithic farming communities, it is evident that it continued to take place – at least on some level – in parts of Britain during the Copper Age. Of course, the famous Beaker culture casts a long shadow over the latter half of the third millennium BC in Britain, but to view the Copper Age solely in terms of this culture would be misleading. This is because it is clear that the equally distinctive, indigenous Late Neolithic Grooved Ware culture coexisted for some time alongside the new and radically different one, which originated on the Continent. Although there is undeniably much more to these two cultures than the striking Grooved Ware and Beaker vessels that are often seen as their hallmarks, there can be little doubt that these decorated pots were of considerable importance to the people who made them. Thus, what these pots may have been used for, and what they may tell us about their respective makers, will be discussed in the following chapter. After this, we will delve into the deeply fascinating world of Copper Age 'art', which is a world that is undoubtedly surrounded by a great air of mystery. Next, our attention will be turned to the famous ritual and ceremonial monuments of Copper Age Britain and the less spectacular, but nonetheless equally as interesting evidence relating to settlement and subsistence during this time. We conclude with the darker side of life in the British Copper Age, and material from the archaeological record that is indicative of the occurrence of warfare during this period will be discussed. Some may not agree that 'true' warfare existed during the prehistoric period in general, and prefer instead to talk of such things as 'feuding' or 'inter-personal violence', but whatever your viewpoint is in this respect, there is no escaping the fact that in the prehistoric period, people killed each other in armed conflicts.

THE INCEPTION OF
THE COPPER AGE

It is this sudden accumulation of distinctive traits that makes it difficult to believe that the Beaker 'package' was no more than the chance convergence of native traditions … It is unlikely that all this, like Topsy, just 'grow'd' rather than being introduced into Britain as the customs and possessions of a continental society.

(Burl 1989: 110)

In Britain, the mid-third millennium BC marked the beginning of the end for the old world of the Neolithic (a world that had lasted for some fifteen hundred years). Around 2500 BC, a novel and distinctive way of life, or 'culture', began to take root here. The main characteristics of this culture were: 'the use of metal and the know-how to extract copper and gold; a new, international style of pottery and potting techniques; fancy archery gear; continental dress fashions; the use of domesticated, pony-sized horses; and a way of dealing with the dead that emphasised the individual, often portraying men as heroic hunters or warriors' (Sheridan 2008: 27).

For a large part of the twentieth century, the archaeological consensus was that these significant changes in Late Neolithic society could be attributed to the famous 'Beaker people' who arrived in Britain from the Continent, either as peaceful immigrants, or as warlike invaders who conquered its indigenous Neolithic communities. Similar thinking was also applied to other important periods in British prehistory and the inception of the Neolithic or the Iron Age provides us with two notable examples. This approach to the interpretation of British prehistory was undoubtedly stimulated by the German archaeologist, Gustav Kossina. In the late nineteenth century, influenced by the work of earlier German 'migrationists', Kossina developed the study of culture history in European archaeology (Anthony 1990: 896; Shennan 1987: 366). Essentially, his romantic and nationalistic view of European prehistory was that the spread of distinct archaeological material throughout Europe revealed the migration of actual ethnic groups or peoples (*ibid.*). It may also be interesting to note that Kossina's 1912 work, *Die Deutsche Vorgeschichte, eine Herrvoragend Nationale Wissenschaft* (German Prehistory, a Supremely National Science) later became an indispensable part of official Nazi mythology (Adams, Van Gerven & Levy 1978: 493). Kossina's approach to the interpretation of cultural change in European prehistory was taken up and refined by the renowned twentieth-century Australian archaeologist, V. Gordon Childe, and 'in [his] hands it became a powerful instrument for the reconstruction of European prehistory' (Anthony 1990: 896). As has been further said (Adams, Van Gerven & Levy 1978: 493) of Childe, '[he was] [t]he real organizing genius of European migrationism [and] his lead was soon followed all over the world by those analyzing and writing about prehistory'. Unsurprisingly, then, migrations and invasions came to occupy a central position in mainstream British archaeology and the 'culture-historical' school dominated archaeological thinking for many years.

However, with the rise to dominance of the Anglo-American 'New', or 'Processual' archaeology in the late 1960s, the idea that migrations and invasions lay behind cultural change was strongly attacked and, as a result, fell markedly out of favour in Britain. The origins of the 'New Archaeology' lay in two highly influential works, published in 1968 – *New Perspectives in Archaeology* and *Analytical Archaeology* – which were written by the American scholar Lewis R. Binford and the British scholar David L. Clarke, respectively; both authors urging for a revolution in archaeological theory (Dark 1995: 8–9). As John Chapman (1997: 12) has noted, '[a]n important part of the New Archaeology was an attempt at scientific rigour and explanatory factors for cultural change such as internal social differentiation, environmental change and population replaced migration and invasion for almost two decades' (*ibid.*). The New Archaeologists were undoubtedly justified in their rejection of the simplistic, migrationist and invasionist models of the culture historical school, which gave indigenous people little part to play in cultural change (Brodie 1994: 3). Indeed, there is certainly more than a little truth in Grahame Clark's (1968: 172) famous accusation that British archaeologists of the earlier twentieth century had suffered from an 'invasion neurosis' that was rooted in Britain's imperial past, and which even led them to see vague similarities in British and continental artefacts as evidence of cultural contact and invasion (it should be noted though, that Clark still adhered to the idea that the appearance of the Beaker culture was the result of some level of immigration from the Continent). However, while arguments such as Clark's carried some weight, it has been suggested by Chapman (1997: 17) that the 'generational experiences' of British and American archaeologists had a significant part to play in influencing the rise of the New Archaeology. As he has plausibly argued (*ibid.*), unlike many of their European counterparts, they had not lived through the invasions, mass movements of people, and the accompanying violence and violation that were part and parcel of life in continental Europe during the First and Second World Wars.

With this major theoretical shift in archaeological interpretation it was only a matter of time before the Beaker people were virtually erased from the pages of prehistory and for much of the later twentieth century they were reduced to an archaeological 'package', with archaeologists favouring the idea that this package was adopted for various reasons by Late Neolithic communities in Britain. Particularly influential in this respect was the series of papers written by Stephen

Shennan in the late 1970s, in which he argued that Beaker assemblages in Central Europe were not spread by migrating Beaker groups (see Price *et al.* 1998; 2004 for evidence that casts considerable doubt on Shennan's theory), but rather, were adopted as markers of prestige or status (Brodie 1998: 43). However, in the late 1980s, the question of migration re-emerged on the archaeological agenda (Anthony 1997: 21) and as a result, the voices of some scholars (e.g. Brodie 1994; 1998) began to be raised against the prevailing view regarding the introduction of the Beaker culture into Late Neolithic Britain. Although these prehistorians were not advocating a return to the large-scale invasions and migrations of the earlier twentieth century, they argued that the idea of the novel and innovative Beaker culture being brought to Britain by small groups of Beaker immigrants should be seriously considered (or 'reconsidered' – in his works Childe had favoured the idea that bands of Beaker people had roamed through Europe in search of land and raw materials). Of course, just as contemporary society is likely to have impacted on the archaeological thinking of the New Archaeologists, so too it may have influenced those who argued for the return of the Beaker people, and other possible examples of immigration/invasion in prehistoric Europe. As Chapman (1997: 18) has noted, it could perhaps be argued that the huge numbers of Eastern European refugees entering Western Europe in the late 1980s (after the fall of the Berlin Wall), and the exaggerated media coverage of these large-scale movements, had an impact on archaeological thinking. Whatever the truth is in this respect, undoubtedly, we would be naïve to believe that the contemporary world does not influence academic ideas about those of the distant past. However, as will be seen in this chapter, there is a growing body of archaeological evidence strongly suggesting that the innovations which appeared in prehistoric Britain *c.* 2500 BC were indeed brought by continental Beaker immigrants.

We will turn first to Scotland, as several early Beaker graves found here have provided strong hints that some of the first Beaker people to arrive in Britain from overseas were 'Dutch'. It is also possible that these people were travelling from the homeland of the Beaker culture, as the Low Countries – and in particular, the Dutch Veluwe area – have often been seen to play a highly significant part in the origin of the Beaker Culture (Vander Linden in Sarauw 2008: 27). However it has also been argued (Case 2007) that this should be sought in the Tagus Estuary of Portugal, rather than in the Lower Rhine, but it is not my intention to get bogged down in what is obviously a complex issue that may never be fully resolved.

'Dutch' Beaker Immigrants in Scotland?

Upper Largie

The first grave to be considered here is the example discovered in 2005 in advance of quarrying at Upper Largie (Sheridan 2008b), which lies in the west of Scotland in the Kilmartin Valley – an area famed for its fine and abundant collection of prehistoric monuments. The grave consisted of a large sub-rectangular or bath-

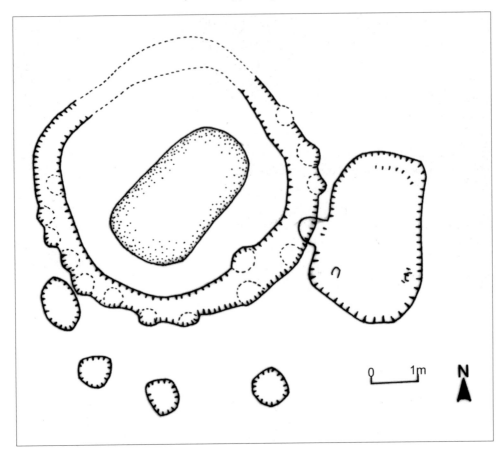

1. Plan of Upper Largie Beaker grave. (Redrawn after Sheridan)

shaped pit (aligned NE–SW) surrounded by a ring ditch (1) and a dark-brown, damp organic deposit found in its interior probably represented the rotted remains of a plank-built wooden burial chamber, or coffin. A layer of rounded cobbles and flattish stones were found above this deposit and it seems likely that these had once formed a small cairn over the burial chamber or coffin. At the bottom of the pit, three damaged yet distinctive Beakers were discovered: two were of the 'Maritime' type while the other was an 'All-Over-Cord' Beaker (2). In addition to the Beakers, a small flint knife and flint fabricator or 'strike-a-light' (both of which showed signs of use), were found near the AOC Beaker. As its name suggests, the latter tool would have been used for sparking fires into life and it is felt that they were used in conjunction with lumps of iron pyrites. Several radiocarbon dates were obtained from pieces of charcoal found in the grave, and in the ring ditch, and these placed it in the twenty-fifth or twenty-fourth century BC.

Within the fill of the ditch, mostly on its outer edge, were fifteen post-holes that appeared to mark the remnants of some sort of wooden enclosure. An arc of four larger post holes stood just outside the ditch to the south, although whether

2. AOC Beaker and Maritime Beaker from Upper Largie. (Alison Sheridan)

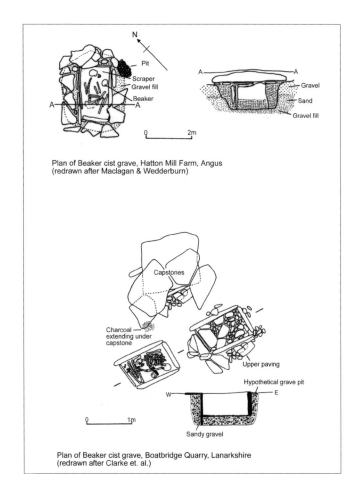

3. Plans of Scottish cist graves.

these were contemporary with the Beaker burial, or associated with the other sub-rectangular pit cut into the eastern edge of the ring ditch, was unclear. Although as with its close neighbour, no human remains were found in this secondary pit, it was felt that this too had contained a chamber or coffin. The presence of a unique footed Food Vessel (dated to *c.* 2160–2080 BC) in the pit, which showed the influence of both Irish and Yorkshire potters, pointed to its use as grave. Intriguingly, ten pebbles were found inside this pot and it could be that they were charms or talismans of some sort – perhaps deposited by the mourners to protect the deceased from malevolent spirits. Such ideas could of course be dismissed as mere flights of fancy, but collections of pebbles and stones have been found at other prehistoric ritual and funerary monuments in Britain. Therefore, it seems highly likely that these mysterious deposits did have a 'magical' purpose of some sort.

Whether the Upper Largie grave represents the final resting place of an immigrant from the Netherlands can, unfortunately, never be known, as there was no trace of the body that had been laid in this grave some four and a half thousand years ago. If skeletal remains had survived, scientific analysis of the person's teeth may have given an indication of their birthplace. Basically, this analysis involves the examination of strontium and oxygen isotopes, which become locked into a person's tooth enamel and bones through ingesting water and food, and these can provide a chemical 'fingerprint' for the area/s in which they lived. It should be pointed out, however, that although isotope analysis may give us a good idea of a person's birthplace, it cannot pinpoint exactly where this was and can only provide us with possibilities in this regard (Janet Montgomery pers. comm.). Nonetheless, at the least, the Upper Largie grave does provide firm evidence of links between Scotland and the Netherlands at the beginning of the Copper Age in the mid-third millennium BC, and the first indication of this is the style of the grave. In Scotland, numerous Beaker burials have been found and these generally consist of simple, stone-lined cist graves sometimes covered with low mounds of earth or stones (3). However, as we have seen, the Upper Largie grave does not conform to this general pattern and in fact, where it finds its strongest parallels is in the Lower Rhine Basin at Dutch sites such as Anlo (*ibid.* 250). In addition to the markedly different nature of the grave, there are the three Beakers to consider, as strikingly similar vessels – both in terms of their decoration and method of manufacture – have been recorded at sites in the Netherlands. In fact, as Alison Sheridan (*ibid.* 251) has remarked, '[the Upper Largie Beakers] could easily be 'lost' among those found in the Netherlands'. Thus, all in all, the evidence found at Upper Largie makes it hard to resist the idea that the individual buried here had travelled far from his community in the Netherlands. Furthermore, it also seems unlikely that this 'Dutchman' was 'flying solo', as he (or she) was buried by other people following a continental tradition that was completely new in Late Neolithic Britain (Sheridan 2008a: 64).

Newmill Farm

Another possible – if not probable – example of the burial of a Dutch Beaker immigrant comes from the grave discovered accidentally during the emergency excavation of an Iron Age settlement and souterrain at Newmill Farm near Perth (Watkins & Shepherd 1978–80). This grave shows some marked similarities to the Upper Largie example and consisted of a long, shallow, bath-shaped grave-pit (though it was roughly orientated E–W like many of the 'Protruding Foot Beaker' graves from the Netherlands, which belong to the earliest stages of the Beaker culture here) surrounded by the remains of a 'penannular ring ditch' (broken by a gap at one point in its circumference), which had an internal diameter of some 6.3m (4). As at Upper Largie, there may have been some type of circular wooden fence or enclosure that had enclosed the burial, but the evidence for the existence of one (a few ambiguous stakeholes) was not particularly convincing. A number of postholes were also found within the area enclosed by the ditch, but it is perhaps more likely that these represented the remains of structures built by the later Iron Age community. On closer examination of the grave (which was overlain by a low cairn of very large pebbles), it was apparent that it had originally contained a thin U-shaped organic container or coffin, which was almost as long as the grave, though it was hard to say for sure of what material it had been made. Unfortunately, no trace of a body was found, but unlike the grave's occupant a few grave goods had survived the ravages of time and the acidic soil of this area. As at Upper Largie, a used flint strike-a-light and knife (5) were discovered in the grave, but perhaps the most significant find was the unusual and early Dutch-style Beaker, which had a low S-profile and was decorated with a distinctive 'herringbone' pattern (6). Such Beakers are rarely seen in Britain, though they

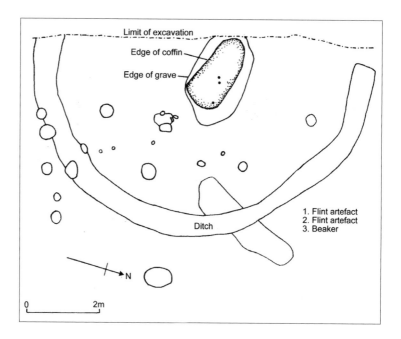

4. Plan of Newmill Beaker grave. (Redrawn after Watkins & Shepherd)

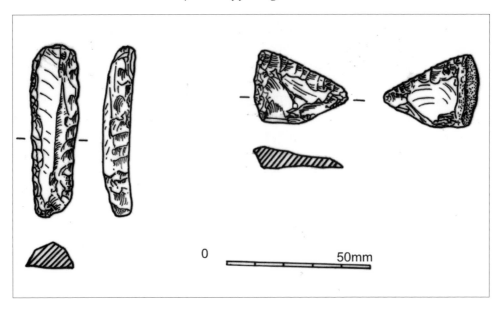

0   50mm

5. Flint 'strike-a-light' and knife from Newmill Beaker grave. (Redrawn after Watkins & Shepherd)

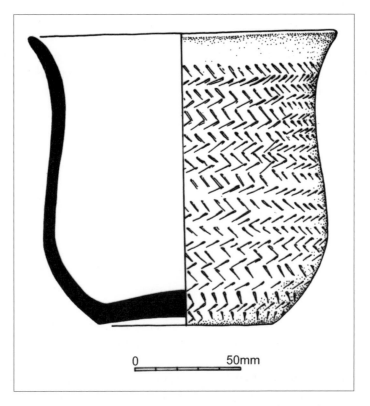

0   50mm

6. Dutch-style Beaker from Newmill. (Redrawn after Watkins & Shepherd)

find very close parallels in Beakers found at Dutch sites such as Bargeroosterveld, Emmen and Soesterberg, and this style of Beaker is felt to date to the primary stage of the development of the Beaker culture in the Netherlands in the late twenty-sixth/early twenty-fifth century BC.

Therefore, as the excavators of the Newmill grave rightly say (*ibid.* 41), 'the continental affinities demonstrated for the grave rituals suggest that Newmill represents more than an exercise in fashion or cult packaging on the part of some of the indigenous late Neolithic inhabitants of Tayside'. In other words, the archaeological evidence found at Newmill points more strongly to immigration rather than 'emulation'. Thus there is a good chance that the individual buried at Newmill was a 'compatriot' of the person buried in the Upper Largie grave.

Sorisdale

The sand dunes near Sorisdale on the north-west coast of the isle of Coll (Inner Hebrides) have produced a rich array of archaeological finds ranging in time from the Mesolithic to the early historic period. Included amongst these finds is an early Beaker grave discovered in 1976 after a series of storms had left the skull of its long-hidden occupant eroding out of the dunes (Ritchie & Crawford 1977–78). Detailed excavation of the site revealed that a simple grave-pit had been dug in the natural sand and cut through a midden that lay next to the eastern end of the remains of an oval-shaped structure that was probably a house (7). Unfortunately, the excavators of the site were not able to determine the exact relationship between the grave, midden, and house, although the midden did contain sherds of plain beaker domestic ware and an almost complete domestic Beaker (8). As Stuart Needham (2005: 182) has pointed out, the appearance of Beaker domestic pottery in association with an early Beaker grave somewhat weakens the argument that the first Beakers to arrive in Britain were the finely made decorated examples that were used as prestige items.

The Sorisdale grave contained the incomplete remains of a young adult (aged 17–25) of unknown sex and a small AOC Beaker (8) had been placed behind his/her head. The survival of skeletal material in the burial proved to be of some importance, as this allowed isotopic analysis to be been carried out on the individual's tooth enamel, as part of the ongoing nationwide Beaker People Project (Sheridan 2008b: 252), which aims to provide answers to the long-debated question of how the Beaker culture emerged in prehistoric Britain. The results of this analysis proved to be extremely interesting as they showed that the Sorisdale individual had not been born on Coll and was definitely not a local (Alison Sheridan pers. comm.). Although at the time of writing, we are still awaiting definitive results in this regard, a possible Dutch birthplace cannot be ruled out (*ibid.*). However, it is quite possible that this individual had not travelled particularly far and he may even have come from another part of the Scottish coastlands (Janet Montgomery pers. comm.). Radiocarbon dates obtained from the skeletal material also put the burial of the Sorisdale individual in a similar time frame to those found at Upper Largie and Newmill, producing a date range of *c.* 2500–2250 BC (*ibid.*).

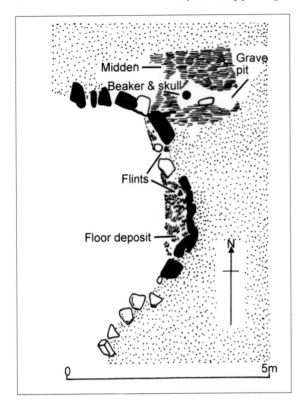

7. Plan of Beaker grave and probable house, Sorisdale Coll. (Redrawn after Ritchie *et al.*)

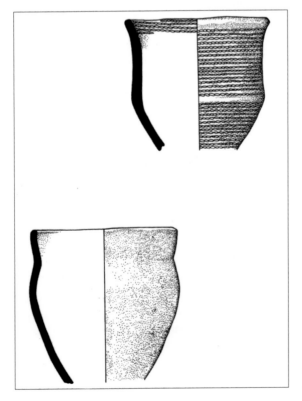

8. AOC Beaker & Domestic Beaker, Sorisdale. (Redrawn after Ritchie *et al.*)

Biggar Common

Further intriguing evidence, pointing towards Dutch Beaker immigrants settling in Scotland at the start of the British Copper Age, has been found at an early Neolithic long mound or barrow located on Biggar Common in Upper Clydesdale, Lanarkshire (Johnston 1997). Excavations at the mound revealed a grave-pit (aligned E–W) ringed by a discontinuous kerb of boulders and partially covered by a small cairn that had been dug into its eastern end. The grave (which contained no remnants of its occupant) closely resembled that found at Newmill and although no traces of a coffin or encircling ring ditch were discovered, these could have been easily missed during the excavations (Sheridan 1997: 223). A finely made, polished stone axe-head, some small flint tools, one agate pebble and a few quartzite pebbles were found in the grave – with the latter perhaps providing further Scottish evidence of the placing of 'magically-charged' stones in prehistoric funerary contexts.

The upper fill of the pit contained a crushed, Maritime-style continental Beaker (9a) and mixed in with the cairn material and the pit-fill was the remains of a small undecorated dish (9b). Lying on the surface of the cairn were sherds from

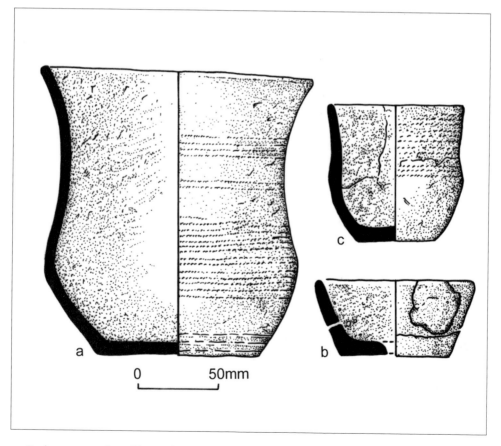

9. Beaker pottery from Biggar Common. (Redrawn after Johnston)

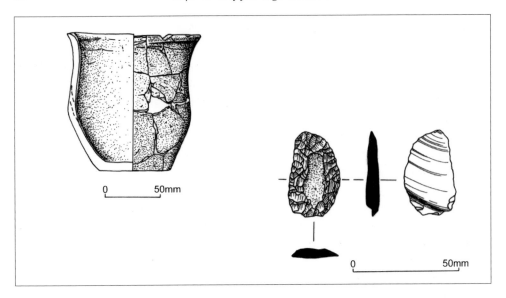

10. Undecorated Beaker and 'slug' knife from Beechwood Park. (Redrawn after Suddaby & Sheridan)

a highly unusual vessel (9c) that would not look out of place among pots of the continental Corded Ware tradition (*ibid*: 216), although it also bore a resemblance to the Protruding Foot Beakers found in the Netherlands (Sheridan 2008b: 251). The discovery of this latter pot sheds some fascinating light on the funerary rituals of Beaker people, as it is evident that it was deliberately smashed (perhaps after a libation ritual?) on the stones of the cairn (Sheridan 1997: 23).

Beechwood Park
Our final Scottish example of a grave that may once have contained a Beaker immigrant from the Netherlands was discovered prior to the development of land at Beechwood Park, Inverness (Suddaby & Sheridan 2006). A sub-rectangular pit aligned east to west came to light during archaeological evaluation of the site and, although no body or traces of a coffin or chamber were found in the pit, a crushed, undecorated Beaker and a small flint knife (10) were found at its base – hinting (but not proving) that the pit had probably also once contained a body. The Beaker had been made using four coils or sections of clay, and it appears that more than one spatula had been used in the shaping of the vessel.

The Beechwood Park Beaker was clearly of an early type (dating to *c.* 2500–2400 BC) and although lacking decoration, closely resembled AOC Beakers from the Lower and Middle Rhine. Perhaps of even greater interest was the fact that it had been shaped using spatulae – a technique that can be seen with several continental Beakers, but as yet, not on Scottish, or other British Beakers (*ibid*. 84). Perhaps then, the individual who may have been buried at Beechwood Park was a specialist immigrant potter, and a pot they made in life accompanied them in death.

Other Possible Beaker Immigrant Graves

In addition to the above Scottish evidence, other Beaker graves from Britain point in the direction of immigrants arriving from overseas in the Early Copper Age, and the first to be mentioned is the example discovered at Talbenny, Pembrokeshire (Fox 1942). This grave provided intriguing signs that it was not just Scotland that saw the arrival of Beaker groups from the Netherlands during the inception of the British Copper Age. On South Hill, underneath a larger and later burial mound (featuring a cremation in a Collared Urn) of the Early Bronze Age, the site's excavator, Cyril Fox, discovered a Beaker 'grave' (no human remains were found) under a low cairn. This was surrounded by a ring ditch, and the stake holes found within the ditch revealed that a wooden, wattled fence had once stood within it. As has previously been mentioned, a similar enclosure was identified in the Dutch-style grave at Upper Largie and one may also been erected by the people who dug the Newmill grave (Watkins & Shepherd 1980: 41). Interestingly, similar wattle enclosures have been identified at sites in the Netherlands such as Altenrath (ibid.). Within the enclosure at Talbenny, a simply decorated Beaker (11) was placed next to a long and narrow hollow, or pit (c. 6ft long by 2ft wide), which was covered by a low cairn of stones and clay, although no skeletal remains had survived.

Although Fox (1942: 7) remarked that the pit 'seemed to symbolise a grave [and was not] intended for a human body', as Trevor Watkins and Ian Shepherd (1978–80: 40) have noted, a long, narrow pit and low covering cairn were also

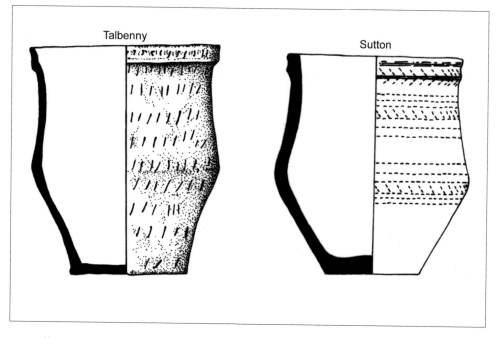

11. Talbenny Beaker (redrawn after Fox) and Sutton Beaker (redrawn after Case).

found at the Newmill grave. Furthermore, a flint knife resembling the one from the Newmill Beaker grave was associated with the primary cairn covering the one at Talbenny. A similar architectural sequence to that at Talbenny was also observed at Sutton, Glamorgan, where an earlier Beaker burial under a low cairn had preceded the larger burial mound and cremation burial that dated to the Early Bronze (Lynch 2000: Fig. 3.15). Cyril Fox (1942: 24) stated that the Beaker found in the primary burial 'was very like that found at South Hill', and whilst the two pots do not seem to be quite as similar as he felt (11) they do both feature cordoned rims, which is also observed on Beakers of the Dutch Veluwe area (Griffiths 1957: 70). Perhaps the most interesting feature of the Sutton Beaker grave, however, was that as at Talbenny; the base of the primary cairn had been deliberately set in a depression that had been dug at a level slightly below the original ground surface and this technique also features in some Dutch Beaker graves (Watkins & Shepherd 1980: 41). It should be mentioned here that Aubrey Burl (1976: 256) also feels that the evidence found at Talbenny may indicate the presence of Beaker immigrants, although he has suggested that they hailed from Germany rather than the Netherlands.

Moving from south-western Wales to southern England, further possible evidence of Beaker immigration may come from the early Beaker grave found at the famous multi-period funerary and ceremonial complex at Barrow Hills, near Radley in Oxfordshire (Barclay & Halpin 1999). In the south-western end of the complex there was a series of Beaker flat graves or burial pits, and in Flat Grave 919 the skeleton of a young child (aged about five), a small amount of cremated bone belonging to a two- to three-year-old, and the skeleton of a newborn baby were found. Radiocarbon dates obtained from the bones of the older child and baby suggest that they were buried c. 2600–2500 BC (Garwood 1999: 294, Figure 9.3; 295, Figure 9.4), which, if correct, places them among the earliest Beaker burials from Britain. Two Beakers that are not easily paralleled among British Beakers (Needham 1999: 327) were found in the grave and the 'barbed wire' decoration' seen on the smaller pot was a technique widespread on the North European Plain (*ibid.*). Of even greater interest, perhaps, were the three copper rings that were found near the oldest child and although these must have been ornaments of some kind, it seems unlikely that they were worn by the child as their maximum diameters, which lay between 17 and 21 mm, seem to argue against this (Brück 2004: 314). Although the ultimate source of the metal from which the rings were made is unknown, it remains possible that the rings had been carried a very long way from this source before they were finally placed in Grave 919 (Northover 1999: 193). In other words, these copper rings could have been carried by a Beaker group who had travelled to Britain from the Continent and perhaps it is even possible that the child who was buried with them arrived as part of this group.

Another interesting grave at Barrow Hills was the one discovered beneath Barrow 4A, which contained an adult male (probably aged around twenty-five to thirty-five years) who had been laid in a rectangular-shaped pit surrounded by a ring ditch (Barclay & Halpin 1999). Accompanying him were a fine pair of gold basket earrings or hair tresses (plate 1) and a large, 'European style' Beaker which also featured a cordoned rim. Although we can only speculate as to the significance of this grave, there may be hints that it contained an immigrant. Firstly, the fact that the ring ditch was only 2.5 feet wide by 1 foot deep suggests that rather than being a quarry ditch, it represented a foundation trench for a circular fence or screen or some sort (Clarke 1970: 76), and thus we may possibly have another Dutch-style Beaker grave. Secondly, and maybe more importantly, there are the artefacts to consider; the Beaker bears comparison with the 'Dutch' Beakers found at Talbenny and Sutton and 'has good Rhineland parallels' (*ibid.*), and the earrings/hair tresses, which are rare in Britain, belong to the earliest phase of Beaker goldworking (Fitzpatrick 2003: 151). It is felt that the latter represent an insular British tradition, which ultimately took its lead from prototypes in continental Europe (Taylor in Healy 1999: 327), although this does not necessarily mean that those who wore them were 'British'. A very similar pair of earrings/hair tresses was found in the rich Beaker grave at Chilbolton, Hampshire (Russell 1990) and like their Barrow Hills counterparts, they find an interesting parallel with a pair from a Corded Ware Grave found at Wasosz, Poland (Taylor 1994: 57). As will be seen below, another similar pair of gold earrings/hair tresses was also discovered with Britain's most famous Beaker immigrant. The radiocarbon dates obtained from the man buried beneath Barrow 4A, and his accompanying grave goods, indicate that he died in the earlier part of the Copper Age, around 2400 BC (Garwood 1999: 294, Figure 9.3; 295, Figure 9.4).

Unfortunately (or not, depending on your point of view), the Beaker People Project was unable to gain access to the skeletal material from Barrow Hills (Mike Parker Pearson pers. comm.), and so, for the present, any clues to the origins of the occupants of the above graves will remain locked in the ancient remains of their bodies.

Another early Beaker grave from England that is perhaps also worth considering is the richly furnished example discovered in 1996 during a salvage excavation at Wellington Quarry in Herefordshire (Harrison, Jackson & Napthan 1999). The grave consisted of an irregular oval pit that was perhaps timber-lined and the deceased (who was probably a male) appears to have been laid on his side in a crouched position with his head pointing to the north-east. Accompanying the deceased were four barbed and tanged arrowheads, three arrowhead 'blanks', three well-made flint knives, two triangular flint points/daggers, a finely made and decorated Maritime AOO (All Over Ornamented) Beaker of the 'Herringbone' variety, the corroded remains of a tanged copper knife, and a fragment of a finely made stone wrist guard (12). The wrist guard may have been deliberately broken or ritually 'killed' before the burial and it is even possible that it was a treasured heirloom. The copper knife lay in the centre of the grave, although it was in a very fragmentary condition and only consisted of a few traces of metal and dark stains in the ground. Its position in the middle of the grave indicates that it may have been worn on the waist of the dead man as he was placed in the grave. Such

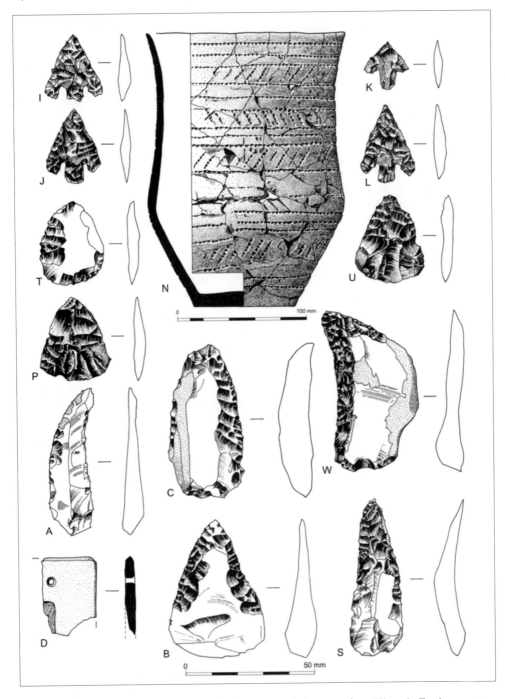

12. Artefacts from Wellington Quarry Beaker grave. (Worcestershire Historic Environment and Archaeology Services)

knives are felt to be among the earliest metal objects in Britain and are not very common in Beaker graves. Its occurrence in the grave along with the fine Beaker and other grave goods suggest that the deceased was of some status; they may also perhaps indicate that the Wellington Quarry grave marked the burial place of an immigrant. As the excavators (*ibid.*: 15) of the Wellington Quarry grave say: '[i]t is not impossible that the tanged knife and wrist guard were artefacts made on the Continent and imported to the UK'. Of course, these artefacts could well have travelled along some sort of far-reaching exchange/trading network, but it is equally possible that the knife and wrist guard were 'imported' as prized possessions by an arrival (who was perhaps a leader of some sort) from overseas who actually wore them about his person. The almost complete lack of human remains in the grave meant that its date could not be assessed scientifically, but its excavators felt that on the basis of the decorative style of the Beaker, it was dug *c.* 2750–2550 BC. If this date is correct, the Wellington Beaker burial undoubtedly ranks as one of the earliest – if not *the* earliest – Beaker grave yet found in Britain.

Beaker Immigrants in Wessex

Of course, while there is a good chance that the Scottish and Welsh Beaker burials mentioned briefly above mark the final resting places of Dutch Beaker immigrants, we have no conclusive proof of this. There is even less certainty that the English Beaker graves also briefly examined represent the burial places of continental arrivals, and it may be, rather, that they indicate contact between Britain and the Continent in the mid-third millennium BC. However, the same cannot be said when we turn to an individual who has been labelled the 'poster boy' of the Copper Age (Mullin 2008: 6), or, to give him his more familiar epithet, the 'Amesbury Archer'. Since the discovery of his grave in 2002, the Amesbury Archer has undoubtedly become one of Britain's most famous prehistoric residents and no doubt many readers will know something of his fascinating story, but his significance means that he cannot be excluded from the pages of this book.

The Amesbury Archer and his 'Companion'

This famous Beaker immigrant was discovered in May 2002 during the building of a new school on Boscombe Down, near the small market town of Amesbury in Wiltshire, which lies about 3 miles from Stonehenge (Burl 2007; Fitzpatrick 2002; 2003; 2009). As yet, the Archer's grave has provided us with the richest Beaker burial from Britain and it would be surprising (though not impossible) if another Beaker grave of this quality came to light. Excavation of the grave suggested that the Archer had been laid to rest in a wooden mortuary chamber or coffin and, as with several other Beaker burials in southern Britain, this may have been covered by a small earthen mound. Analysis of the Archer's bones showed that at his time of death he had been aged around thirty-five to forty-five years old. In our society, the Archer would not have been considered old, but in the Copper Age he was probably seen as something of an 'elder'. Archaeology has shown that most people in Chalcolithic Britain (and prehistoric Britain in general) would have lived much shorter lives in comparison to our own all-too-brief ones and that hardship and disease were familiar bedfellows. In fact, it is apparent that the Amesbury Archer would have had to put up with considerable suffering in his later years, as he had an terrible abscess on his jaw (that would have been very painful and would also have given him very bad breath) and a few years before his death, virtually all of his left knee-cap had somehow been ripped off. This terrible injury would not only have caused him to walk with a straight left leg that swung out to his side; as a result, he also had an infection in his bones that would have caused him constant pain. How this awful injury occurred will remain unknown, but it may have been as a result of a riding accident as it is felt that Beaker people could have ridden small horses (similar to those ridden by some Native American peoples), although there is no firm evidence of this in Britain. It is perhaps also possible that this traumatic injury was meted out to him by another individual, perhaps even in combat, although admittedly it is in a somewhat strange place in this respect.

Leaving aside the harsh reality of life in Copper Age Britain, and the Archer's suffering, we will turn briefly to the beautiful and intriguing objects that were buried with him. Included among the grave goods were five early Beakers (one AOC type and two others decorated with plaited cord – also uncommon in Britain), two gold basket earrings/hair tresses (quite possibly made in Britain from continental ore), three copper knives of Spanish and French origin, fifteen finely made barbed and tanged arrowheads, two archer's bracers or wrist guards, four boars' tusks, numerous flint tools and a 'cushion' stone that was probably used for making small items of copper and gold. The quality and quantity (around 100 items) of the Archer's grave assemblage indicated that he must have been a man of considerable standing in the Stonehenge region. Interestingly, radiocarbon dates on his body revealed that he was buried between 2470 and 2280 BC, which was when Stonehenge may have been transformed into the mighty monument of stone that is so familiar around the world today. Thus it is not inconceivable that he had a significant part to play in its transformation and perhaps the title given to him by the press – the 'King of Stonehenge' – is not that far from the truth; although we would perhaps expect him to be buried a little closer to the site if he was indeed a major force behind its construction? Also, it should be pointed out that it has recently been plausibly argued (Parker Pearson *et al.* 2007: 626) that Stonehenge was actually built between 2600 and 2470 BC, which places the arrival of the Amesbury Archer in Britain *after* its construction. King of Stonehenge or not, isotope analysis of the Archer's teeth revealed that he had travelled thousands of miles from his homeland to end his days in Wiltshire. This analysis was carried out by Carolyn Chenery of the British Geological Survey at Keyworth and by Paul Budd at Durham University, and the results revealed that he lived in a colder climate as a child, somewhere in the Alpine Region of Central Europe, with Germany, Switzerland or Austria emerging as strong candidates for his place of birth.

The intriguing grave (Burl 2007; Fitzpatrick 2003; 2009; Mckinley 2011) that was discovered only about 5m away from the Archer's must also be noted here. This was dated to 2460–2140 BC and contained the skeleton of a younger man in his early twenties, who had been buried with flint tools, two boars' tusks and a pair of earrings/hair tresses similar to the Archer's. The proximity of the graves and the fact that they both contained these distinctive and rare gold ornaments indicated some kind of familial link between the two men and recent scientific analysis of their bones appears to confirm this. As Jackie Mckinley (2011: 17–18) tells us, 'these two men share a rare non-metric skeletal variation which shows high hereditability within immediate families and over several generations within a family. This takes the form of a non-osseous 'calcaneonavicular coalition', i.e. a fibrous joint between two of the tarsal (foot) bones seen in only 2.0–2.1% of modern and Medieval European populations'. In addition to this highly suggestive evidence, both men also had similarly shaped 'brachycranial' (round-headed) skulls, were of a similar height (*c.* 5'8"–5'10"), and generally shared similar proportions in their skeletal measurements. It could be, then, that the Archer and his companion were actually a father and son who were laid to rest side-by-side in this pleasant corner of southern England, or alternatively, an uncle and nephew. However, even though it seems highly likely that the two men were somehow related to one another, it is also quite possible that the Archer died many years before his companion was born.

Whether these two important individuals from the distant past were ever involved in the construction of Stonehenge seems unlikely, but they must surely have been aware of its presence, and together, they may well have visited the monument on several occasions to witness and participate in the important ceremonies and rituals that took place there. However, the monument that was found close to their graves could have been of more importance to them than the mighty ring of stone, which stood looming on Salisbury Plain some three miles away. This consisted of a large pit circle, measuring some 63m in diameter, which appears to have been in use from the Late Neolithic to the Early Bronze Age, as evidenced by the discovery of sherds from Grooved Ware, Beakers and Collared Urns. Ramps seen on the sides of four of the larger pits also reveal that these pits held large wooden posts, although for how long is unknown (Wessex Archaeology 2009).

The Boscombe Bowmen

Although less spectacular in terms of the grave goods found within, and not producing a prehistoric 'celebrity', the early Beaker grave (Fitzpatrick 2004; Evans, Chenery & Fitzpatrick: 2006; Burl 2007; Mckinley 2011) found less than half a kilometre from that of the Amesbury Archer proved no less remarkable in the window that it opened onto Beaker migration in the Early Copper Age – although as we will see, there is some uncertainty as to whether it indicates migration into Wessex from north-western Britain, or from continental Europe. Again, many readers are probably familiar with this discovery, but as with the Amesbury Archer, its importance means that it cannot be left out of this book.

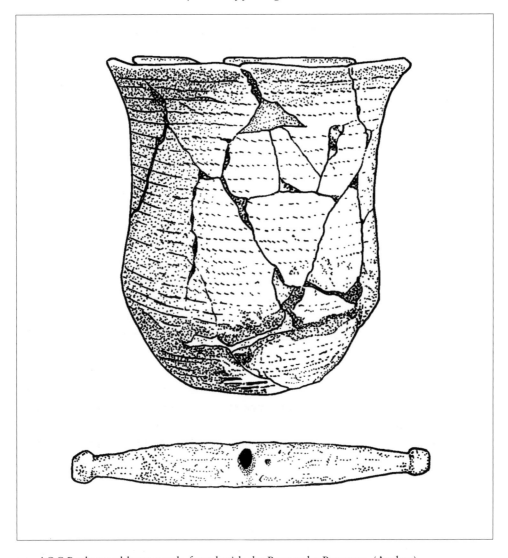

13. AOC Beaker and bone toggle found with the Boscombe Bowmen. (Author)

The grave (dated *c.* 2400 BC) was discovered during an archaeological watching brief at Boscombe Down airfield where a new water pipe was being laid; it contained the bones of seven people: three adult males, a teenager, and three children. The oldest man was aged between thirty and forty-five, and it seems that he may also have walked with a limp because he had badly broken his thighbone at some point in his life. It is possible that, as with the Archer, this injury occurred because the man had fallen off a horse moving at speed. The three children had been buried near his head. The youngest of these was aged around two to four, although little remained of his/her cremated remains, while the other two children were aged about five to six and six to seven years respectively. The teenager was probably male and had been aged about fifteen to eighteen at death and the other two men seem to have died aged between twenty-five and thirty. It also possible that that the bodies of the younger men and the teenager had been exposed to the elements before being placed in the grave (it could be that they were placed on some type of mortuary scaffold). Although it appears to be the case that not all the burials are contemporary, and that some two hundred years may lie between the first and last burial placed in the grave, it is still quite possible that its occupants all belonged to one family.

The grave was very unusual in that collective burials are more typical of the earlier Neolithic period in Britain, and it has produced the largest amount of individuals yet known from a British Beaker grave. It also contained the largest amount of Beakers yet found in a Beaker grave and these pointed to continental connections, with six Beakers of the now familiar early AOC type; one decorated with plated cord and the other perhaps decorated with a combination of corded and combed decoration (13). Also found in the grave where a boar's tusk, flint tools, five barbed and tanged arrowheads and a bone toggle (13), which are very rare in Britain (only one other has been found in Britain, in a rich Beaker burial at Barnack, Cambridgeshire). The presence of the arrowheads in the grave led to the men in the grave being dubbed the 'Boscombe Bowmen'.

Isotopic analysis of the Bowmen's teeth painted another remarkable but somewhat uncertain picture of prehistoric migration in Early Chalcolithic Britain. This revealed that they had been brought up in one place but had subsequently moved to another place aged around six, where they stayed until about the age of thirteen. Later in their lives they moved to the Stonehenge region, where they spent the remainder of their lives, and the analysis of their teeth suggested that the Boscombe Bowmen could well have been born in Wales, or the Lake District. Intriguingly, the famous Stonehenge bluestones, which many archaeologists feel were amazingly hauled some 250km from the Preseli Hills in North Pembrokeshire, may have been erected around the same time as the Bowmen were buried. However, whilst this remains a possibility, there is perhaps a better chance that the Bowmen actually came from somewhere in France, as collective burials (in caves, pit-graves and earlier Neolithic tombs) with associated Beaker artefacts are commonly found in France (Chambon 2004: 70). In fact, examination of their isotopes suggests that an origin in Brittany or the Massif Central are possible for the Bowmen (Evans *et al.* 2006: 318) and it has been suggested (Parker Pearson & Sheridan in Burl 2007: 299) that the isotopes point most strongly towards the former. However, while Brittany is perhaps the likeliest place of origin for the Bowmen, neither can we totally rule out the possibility that they came from south-east Ireland, Portugal, or even the Black Forest region of Germany (Evans *et al.* 2006: 318). It should also be pointed out that it has been argued (Parker Pearson *et al.* 2007: 636) that just as the Amesbury Archer was not involved in the construction of Stonehenge because this happened before he was born, so too the Bowmen cannot have been involved in the erection of the bluestones because these monoliths had also already been standing for many decades before they were buried in their intriguing grave. However, whatever the true date of the arrival of the bluestones at Stonehenge, as we will see later, there is fascinating evidence which strongly suggests that these fascinating monoliths were indeed brought from south-west Wales.

Beaker Migration: Suggestions

As it is clear that metal was important in Beaker society – or at least to those members of its society who were able to signal their status through the use of copper and gold objects – it is possible that one of the main motivations behind early (and later) Beaker migration into Britain was the search for copper ore and gold sources. This is an old idea that sprang from the earlier culture-historical school, but whether the search for metals actually had a significant part to play in driving Beaker migration has recently been questioned (Needham 2007: 42). Nonetheless, it is a theory that still has some merit, and it is conceivable that small-scale continental Beaker groups arrived on British shores intent on 'building a domestic and/or international trade in metals' (Taylor 1994: 58), although we should be wary of viewing this 'trade' as similar to that which exists between modern industrialised nations. It could be, as Joan Taylor (*ibid.*: 41) has suggested, that the first wave of Beaker 'mineral engineers' or 'prospectors' were subsequently followed by small groups of settlers after these prospectors had reported back their discoveries. A similar process has been observed among agricultural migrants in the Philippines and South-East Asia. Here, advance scouts would relay back information on social conditions and resources to potential migrants, who could then follow a 'leapfrogging' migration pattern, jumping great distances and bypassing whole regions (Lefferts in Anthony 1990: 902). A more well-known example of this type of migration comes from nineteenth-century North America, where the expansion of migrant farmers was greatly helped by the trapper scouts who had preceded them, examining possible areas of settlement (Anthony 1990: 902–903). It may even be possible that some of the early AOC Beaker sherds found in coastal locations in Britain relate to such scouting activities when Britain was being 'sized-up' as a potential area for settlement by Beaker groups from overseas (Lewthwaite in Brodie 1994: 30).

Although admittedly actual evidence for continental Beaker 'prospectors' or miners in Britain is ambiguous to say the least, that found at Ross Island in south-western Ireland may well tell a different story and this evidence will be looked at in more detail in the next chapter. Among the tenuous scraps of archaeological material that may be connected to immigrant Beaker prospectors in Britain are the many (over seventy) Beaker-style barbed and tanged arrowheads that were found concentrated within small areas on the North Plynlymon moorland in Powys (Peate 1925a; Peate 1925b; Peate 1928). Among this collection were many that Iorwerth C. Peate (1925a: 198) felt were 'remarkably similar to Irish arrowheads', with one arrowhead in particular (14) finding a very close match to

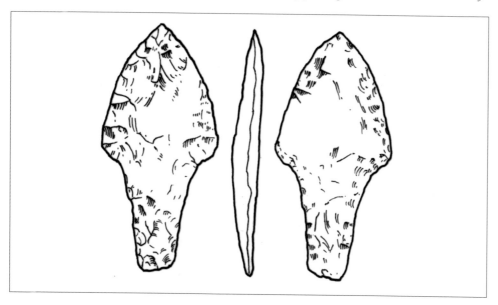

14. Irish-style Beaker arrowhead from North Plynlymon. (Redrawn after Peate)

a type that has been found in various counties of northern Ireland (Peate 1928: 344). Simon Timberlake (2009: 101–102) has made the interesting suggestion that the distribution of these arrowheads around possible former woodland clearings may be associated with deer hunters from Beaker prospecting groups who passed through Wales along the 'metal route' in search of copper ores, and who were in contact with indigenous pastoralists.

Further possible evidence of Copper Age prospectors from Ireland (perhaps belonging to a Beaker group) may be provided by the intriguing tiny stone circle known as 'Circle 275', which lies about 250 yards north-east of the famous 'Druids' Circle' on the moorland of Cefn Coch above the North Welsh coast, near Penmaenmawr (Griffths 1960). This circle comprises of five low but heavy boulders (15) with the lowest and heaviest stone set in the south-western arc of the circle. Aubrey Burl (1999: 40), has noted that Circle 275 closely resembles the five-stone recumbent circles of south-west Ireland, but he has suggested that it represents evidence of 'traders of Irish copper ores bringing the material to north Wales and setting up their own small shrine', rather than prospectors. If this curious monument is an Irish five-stone circle, then it was probably built some time after the first Beaker immigrants had arrived in Britain as these monuments have been dated to *c.* 2200–1500 BC (Burl 2005: 39–48). Aubrey Burl (1976: 256–257) has also suggested that the finely preserved Gors Fawr stone circle (plate 2) in Pembrokeshire may have been used by Beaker immigrants (perhaps of Germanic origin) as a 'trading centre' for stone axes quarried from the nearby Preseli Hills. As will be seen in the next chapter, a small but intriguing object found at the Copa Hill mine in mid-Wales hints that an immigrant Beaker group could lie behind the origin of this fascinating site.

15. Circle 275, Cefn Coch. (Author)

A more recent idea in regard to Beaker migration has been put forward by Neil Brodie (1997). He has suggested that some Late Neolithic groups in Western Europe could have exchanged female marriage partners in return for metallurgists from Beaker groups in Central Europe because they desired copper objects and the knowledge of the 'magical' processes from which these objects sprang. However, it is questionable whether such a scenario can be envisaged for Britain, as there appears to be no material evidence from Late Neolithic Britain found in Beaker contexts on the Continent, which would be expected if women from Britain were moving across the Channel or North Sea, in exchange for continental Beaker metalworkers (*ibid.*: 311).

An interesting theory proposed by Tim Darvill (2007: 151) is that the Amesbury Archer and his companion travelled to Stonehenge because it may have been a renowned healing centre and oracle, where, they believed, their ailments would be cured. Similarly, Alison Sheridan (2008b: 256) has suggested that the Upper Largie individual might have been attracted to the Kilmartin Valley because of the fame of its many sacred sites, or alternatively, because he was seeking copper ore. As Sheridan (2008a: 65) has further noted, the major Wessex monuments and their associated midwinter festivals (e.g. Stonehenge, Avebury) could also have drawn prehistoric 'pilgrims' from the Continent into Britain. Perhaps, then, Stonehenge and other contemporary major ritual and ceremonial sites in Britain were viewed in a similar way to the major Cathedrals of late medieval Europe in the twelfth to fifteenth centuries. These acted as magnets for countless pilgrims from all walks of life who, among other things, came to pray for successful harvests, cures from sickness or disease, safe childbirth, or simply because they wished to give thanks to, or to be close to their god.

Of course, given the complexities of human life, there are likely to have been many other factors behind Beaker immigration into Britain. One possibility in this regard are that some Beaker migrants arrived in Britain because quarrels between kin groups, or political power struggles, had erupted into armed conflict, from which they were fleeing (Brodie 1994: 28). Alternatively, some small continental Beaker groups could have travelled to Britain because they wished to dominate native groups and thus gain power themselves (*ibid.*). It may seem somewhat improbable that such groups could dominate the larger native populations of Late Neolithic Britain, but this process has been noted among several non-state societies and an example from southern Sudan may throw up some interesting possibilities as regards to how Beaker groups might have achieved this.

Here, in the seventeenth century, several small chiefly groups migrated from what is today Uganda and achieved dominance (and the widespread adoption of their language) by a number of means: the importation and display of new and exotic symbols of ritual power; marrying into local populations; bestowing lavish gifts on local leaders; offering military assistance to allies in trouble, or threatening violence to those who were not willing to cooperate (Atkinson in Anthony 1997: 29). This 'elite dominance model' also finds favour among some Anglo-Saxon scholars who argue that the establishment of Anglo-Saxon culture in England had more to do with Romano-British populations adopting significant elements of this culture from a small Anglo-Saxon immigrant elite, rather than the arrival of large numbers of Germanic migrants from the Continent who virtually wiped out the natives (Hamerow 1997; Burmeister 2000: 548).

A final intriguing theory in respect of possible driving forces behind Beaker migration has been noted by Alison Sheridan (2008a: 65). She has pointed out that several archaeologists have proposed that some Beaker immigrants may have been 'heroic' adventurers in the mould of Odysseus or Ulysses, gaining prestige and fame from their brave and daring adventures to far-flung and dangerous places. Perhaps the Amesbury Archer and the Upper Largie 'Dutchman' provide us with examples of such individuals, as visits to the famous sacred sites of Wessex and the Kilmartin Valley would be a natural part of the adventures of these 'hunter-warriors' (*ibid.*).

The Return of the Beaker People

Obviously, we will never know exactly where the Amesbury Archer and the Boscombe Bowmen came from, but they are hugely important figures in the story of the inception of the Copper Age in Britain. Previous to their discovery, there had been rumblings of discontent for some time among British archaeologists who were dissatisfied with the fashionable Beaker 'package' theory, and it is really thanks to the Archer and the Bowmen that this theory began to lose the high ground that it had held for so long. It should also be noted that the likely evidence for Beaker immigration found in Scotland (and Ireland) has also helped in this respect. It will also be interesting to see the final results of the Beaker People Project, as further examples of early Beaker immigrants from the Continent may well be revealed, along with evidence of more 'localised' migration in the Early Copper Age, with indigenous groups who had 'adopted' the Beaker culture moving around the country. In this latter respect, the Beaker People Project has identified a pattern of at least local mobility among Beaker groups on the Yorkshire Wolds, with people moving in and out of the area, perhaps sometimes travelling considerable distances from or to the Wolds (Mandy Jay pers. comm.). One such long-distance traveller identified by the *Beaker People Project* was the adult found in a Beaker burial excavated by J. R. Mortimer at Garton Slack in the nineteenth century, who was 'clearly a long way from home' (Jay & Montgomery 2008: 26). Whether further examples of continental Beaker immigrants will come to light remains to be seen, but one suspects that they will. It seems that the Beaker people who travelled from the Continent (whether as brave and hardy individuals, or in small kin-based groups), and who ushered in a new and exciting period in prehistoric Britain, are beginning to re-emerge from the shadows in which they have been hidden for too long.

2

MINING

Like many other prehistoric people, Britain's earliest copper miners are shadowy figures whose true identities are veiled by the many thousands of years that lie between them and us. Thus it is hard to say for sure whether it was indigenous Late Neolithic communities or immigrant Beaker groups from the Continent who first set in motion mining and metalworking here. However, although it seems very unlikely that we will ever discover who Britain's first copper miners were, evidence found at Ross Island in south-western Ireland strongly indicates, that here at least, a continental Beaker group was behind the first phase of a Copper Age/Early Bronze Age mine complex and associated settlement (c. 2400–1900 BC). The Copper Age mine at Ross Island could also quite possibly be the first one to be worked in Ireland or Britain. Furthermore – and perhaps more importantly – these people have left us with fascinating evidence that throws considerable light on work and domestic life in a Copper Age mining community on the far western edge of Europe.

The Ross Island Copper Age Mine and Beaker Mining Settlement

Ross Island is located among the stunningly beautiful landscapes of the Killarney National Park in south-western Ireland, and is actually a peninsula that juts out from the eastern edge of Lough Leane (16 & plate 3), which is the largest of the famous three lakes of Killarney. The remote beginnings of mining at Ross Island were first recognised by eighteenth-century miners who attributed older mine workings they discovered to 'Danes'; twentieth-century archaeologists also attributed hammer stones found at the site to the Bronze Age. However, it was a team led by William O'Brien of the National University of Ireland, Galway, who uncovered the true significance of the 'Danish' mines during excavations carried out at the site from 1992 to 1996 (O'Brien 2004).

The Danish Mines consist of the 'Western Mine' and the 'Blue Hole' (so called because of its association with the famous 'Blue Men' of local folklore – Cornish miners who worked at Ross Island in the early nineteenth century and whose hair and nails appear to have been turned blue by copper ore contamination) and

16. Aerial view of Ross Island. (William O'Brien)

17. Mine 'cave', western mine area, Ross Island. (William O'Brien)

18. Entrance to lower mine, western mine area, Ross Island. (William O'Brien)

19. Blue Hole mine, Ross Island. (William O'Brien)

these were first recorded on a plan drawn in 1825 by the mining engineer, Thomas Weaver. The Western Mine area features a large, upper mine 'cave' with a curving entrance and a lower mine, which runs eastwards below the former – although for how far is unclear, because only the flooded entrance was discovered during excavations (17, 18). Numerous stone hammers or 'mauls', and animal bones and charcoal were found in the spoil tips that lay in front of the two mine workings. Radiocarbon dates obtained from the charcoal and bones indicated that miners had been extracting copper ore here in the Early Bronze Age *c.* 2200–1900 BC. However, because the excavation team was not able to get into the lower and upper mine because of problems with flooding and concerns over safety (the latter was in real danger of collapsing), it was not possible to find any evidence for earlier mining, though it is known that the Copper Age miners did extract some ore from this area. Unfortunately, it was not possible to excavate the Blue Hole (19) because it is permanently flooded – its water levels fluctuating with those of adjacent Lough Leane. Nevertheless, signs of 'fire-setting' (often associated with ancient, or primitive mining) are evident on its walls, nineteenth-century accounts mention the existence of ancient mine workings here and, most tellingly, copper ore from the Blue Hole was found in both the Copper and Early Bronze Age phases of the associated settlement during the excavations – providing proof of the mine's prehistoric pedigree.

20. Foundations of a Beaker dwelling, Ross Island. (William O'Brien)

The Beaker Mining Settlement

The settlement in which both the Copper Age and Early Bronze Age miners lived and worked at Ross Island lay on the Western Shelf, which is a level escarpment that overlooks the lake. The Copper Age/Early Bronze Age miners were not the first prehistoric people at the site, as the excavations uncovered evidence of Mesolithic activity that may possibly be related to a lakeside camp dating to the latter half of the sixth millennium BC. It also seems that they were not the last miners on the Western Shelf, as two copper smelting furnaces dating to the seventh/eighth century AD were also discovered in this area during excavations.

Turning to the more important Copper Age phase of the mining settlement, radiocarbon dates obtained from various contexts indicated that it was occupied intermittently between *c*. 2400 and 2200 BC and was largely associated with the extraction of copper ore from the Blue Hole mine – although as mentioned above, some ore was also extracted from the Western Mine in this period. Amongst the large corpus of archaeological material recovered was a collection of around four hundred stake-holes and small-post holes, along with several associated trenches. This evidence clearly represented the remains of dwellings in which the first miners at Ross Island had lived, probably on a temporary or seasonal basis. Although we can never say exactly what these structures looked like, their ground plans suggest that they took the form of circular, oval, or sub-rectangular shelters that used bent sapling arrangements for their walls, and vegetation or animal hides as roofing materials (20). The smaller group of shelters had ground plans ranging in size from 4 to 9 sq. m, whilst the larger examples ranged from 11 to 20 sq. m, suggesting that single or small groups of miners lived in them. To modern eyes, such dwellings may seem basic and primitive and not exactly desirable lakeside residences. However, to the people who built and lived in them, they would have been seen as perfectly adequate and even comfortable. They probably also provided focal points around which friends and family gathered to relax after a hard day's work, perhaps in front of a fire, with the beauty of nearby Lough Leane and the Killarney countryside providing a backdrop to their conversation and laughter.

Evidence relating to the food sources that had helped to sustain the miners in their labours was found in the settlement area and took the form of numerous fragments of animal bone. These were identified as belonging to cattle, pig, sheep/goat and a single deer (suggesting occasional hunting trips), although it was clear that the former two species had supplied the miners with the greatest majority of their meat. For the most part, the cattle and pigs (and occasionally sheep or goats) were probably brought to the mining camp trussed up in wooden log boats, but is also possible that some were herded overland from local farming settlements. Surprisingly, considering the mine's location, no evidence of fishing or the hunting of waterfowl was discovered, although this may be because the miners had plentiful food anyway and wished to concentrate on the not inconsiderable task of extracting the copper ore and turning it into a useable metal. It seems likely that several worked cattle ribs and scapulae also found during excavations

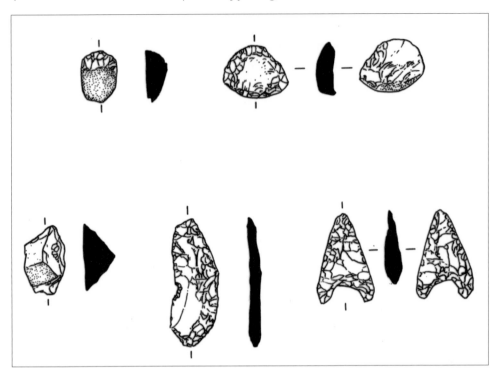

21. Flint tools and arrowhead, Ross Island. (Redrawn after O'Brien)

22. Grinding stone, Ross Island. (William O'Brien)

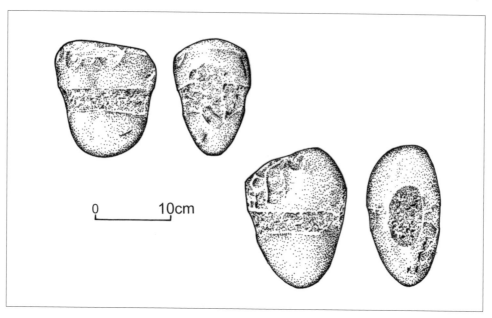

23. Hafted stone hammers, Ross Island. (Redrawn after O'Brien)

24. Mining hammer, Ross Island. (William O'Brien)

25. Lissyviggeen stone circle, near Ross Island. (William O'Brien)

26. Beaker fragments
from Ross Island.
(William O'Brien)

were used as scoops or shovels during the hand-sorting of copper ore within the settlement, and a partial red deer antler may have been used to prise out copper ore from rock-faces weakened by fire-setting – as is suspected at other prehistoric copper mines in Europe (Van Wijngaarden-Bakker 2004).

Undoubtedly, the most intriguing piece of skeletal evidence to be recovered from the Beaker mining settlement was the fragment of a human tibia found in association with a spread of refuse that overlay a trapezoidal Beaker hut. How it had arrived in this rubbish layer will forever remain a Copper Age mystery, but one remote possibility in this respect, is that it relates to an amputation performed on a miner who had been in a serious accident (O'Brien 2004: 475). If such an amputation had been performed, it seems very unlikely that the patient would have survived what would have been an extremely painful and dangerous operation, although the amount of pain may have been combated by the use of herbs and plants with anaesthetic properties, or even alcohol. Perhaps it is more likely that this solitary leg bone represents the remains of a burial disturbed by later activity, although we might expect dead miners to have been buried in their home settlements, rather than what was probably a seasonal settlement (*ibid.*).

Although limited in number, flint tools in the form of scrapers and a plano-convex knife (21) were also found at the site and these were probably related to the processing of meat or animal skins and the manufacture and repair of clothing/equipment made from animal skins (McCartan 2004). In addition to these tools, a hollow-based arrowhead (21) was discovered and the impact fracture seen on its tip revealed that it had been fired at and had hit something; although whether this 'something' was human or animal is not known (the latter is perhaps more likely).

It was not just archaeological material relating to domestic life that was found in the settlement area, but also that which can be linked to the processing of copper ore. Unsurprisingly, hundreds of stone hammers or mauls were found alongside large numbers of anvil slabs and grinding stones (22). The fact that many of these artefacts were broken testifies to their use in conjunction with each other, with the miners using the hammers to crush the ore from the mineralised rock on the anvils or the slabs (it is felt that the latter were used to further refine the ore concentrate before smelting). Many of the stone hammers showed evidence of hafting on their sides (23, 24), pointing to their use in fire-setting operations, which is a technique used by many other ancient and more modern non-state peoples – it has even been recorded in nineteenth-century Europe (O'Brien 1996: 22). Fire-setting basically consists of burning wood fires against a mineralised rock-face in a mine, in order to weaken it prior to pounding it with stone hammers (cold water thrown suddenly onto the rock would also have helped to increase the heat fracturing), which were either hafted or hand-held (*ibid.*). Pits in which the copper ore was smelted were found in the southern part of the site, and although a few pieces of melted copper ore were recovered no actual copper implements were found. It seems that this was because production at the site stopped with copper ingots (two were found during excavations), which were then moved on to settlements in the Killarney area and elsewhere in Ireland (and Britain), where they were cast into finished objects such as axe-heads (William O'Brien pers. comm).

It is also perhaps possible that the Lissyviggeen stone circle (25), which lies about 5 miles from Ross Island, may have been used as a 'place of worship' by its Beaker mining community. This small circle features seven stones surrounded by an inner ditch and outer bank, with two huge outlying stones, and may provide us with an example of a circle-henge, which were built between *c.* 2900–2200 BC (Burl 2005). However, although an excavation was carried out at the site, it was not possible to obtain any secure dates for the circle and so the possibility remains that it represents a later Bronze Age monument that was built inside an earlier Neolithic henge.

Continental Beaker Miners at Ross Island?

As fascinating as the above evidence is, in terms of the door it opens onto the lost world of an Irish mining community of the Copper Age, there can be little doubt that the numerous sherds of Beaker pottery (26) also found at the site marked the most exciting discovery, as they showed that it was Beaker people who had first mined copper ore at Ross Island. The sherds represent the remains of around two dozen early Beakers, the majority of which were simply decorated vessels that, for the most part, were contemporary with the Copper Age phase of mining at Ross Island (Brindley 2004). It is highly likely that the Beakers were used by the miners as domestic drinking vessels and water containers (*ibid.*), and in some cases, they may have been used to wash roasted copper ore from furnace ashes, as suggested by the discovery of Beaker sherds in a shallow pit that was probably associated with this activity. These broken pieces of pottery may have been rather unremarkable in appearance, but their importance cannot be underestimated, because as Paul Budd (2000: 16) has pointed out, they confirmed the long-suspected connection between Beaker users and the introduction of metalworking in many parts of Europe.

Whether these Beaker sherds revealed that a continental Beaker group lay behind the first phase of copper mining at Ross Island is perhaps open to question, as it is conceivable that Beakers were used by local Late Neolithic groups during this time (O'Brien 2004: 565). However, whilst it is quite possible that Beaker pottery was introduced into the wider Killarney area because its indigenous communities were involved in a far-reaching Beaker exchange network, it seems very unlikely that it was local Beaker users who were ultimately responsible for opening up the first copper mine at Ross Island (although it is quite possible that local people did work in some capacity at the mine). As has been plausibly argued by O'Brien (*ibid.*: 563), '[t]he technological processes involved in metal production are too complex to be transmitted orally or by casual contact [and] would certainly have required a movement of specialist metalworkers or some small-scale migration of metal-using groups from the Continent'.

In a similar vein, it has been argued (Roberts *et al.* 2009: 1018) that the evidence for the independent invention of metalworking in Western Europe is slight and that the successful transfer of metallurgical know-how to non-metal-using societies would have required the movement of experienced metalworkers who could then have imparted their skills and knowledge to the former, if they so desired (it seems likely that not all prehistoric metalworkers would have been willing to give up their secrets as some level of social power must have been conferred on those were able to transform rock into metal).

Also, although the scale and complexity of the underground workings during the first phase of mining at Ross Island are admittedly unclear, it has also been pointed out (Ottaway 2001: 91) that the underground mining of ore and its safe and successful extraction requires the presence of highly experienced specialists. Furthermore, and perhaps most tellingly, the miners at Ross Island seem to have deliberately targeted the site because it contained arsenic-rich ores of the *fahlerz* type, which allowed for greater metal yields and eased the smelting process (O'Brien 555). This not only provides us with a further indication of the metallurgical expertise of the Ross Island miners, but the production of arsenical copper at the mining settlement can also be viewed as part of a wider tradition common among Beaker communities in Atlantic Europe (*ibid.* 561).

All in all then, rather than revealing the presence of an enterprising Late Neolithic community who were several technological steps ahead of many of their counterparts in Ireland and Britain, it seems more likely that the fascinating evidence found at Ross Island can be attributed to continental Beaker prospectors (perhaps from the Morbihan area of Brittany) whose long-ranging search for copper ore ended successfully in this beautiful corner of south-western Ireland.

Possible Copper Age Mines in Britain

Copa Hill

It was during the eighteenth and nineteenth centuries when Welsh miners were extracting copper and other ores to help drive the industrial revolution, that there were many discoveries of 'old men's workings', which were often attributed to Roman or medieval miners (O'Brien 1996: 42). Evidence of fire-setting and stone hammers was often found at these earlier mines and although in some cases, it is evident that the later miners were not wrong in their assumptions regarding these earlier mines, modern archaeological investigations have revealed that many of these sites date to the Bronze Age. In fact, it is apparent that Wales was a major region of copper production, particularly in the first half of the Early Bronze Age *c.* 2000–1700 BC and it also evident that mid-Wales (Ceridgion and West Montgomeryshire) occupied a position of some importance as at least twelve Early Bronze Age mines have been identified here (Timberlake 2009: 107). The most thoroughly investigated of these mines is that found on Copa Hill, which lies about 20km to the east of Aberystwyth in the upper reaches of the Ystwyth Valley, Ceredigion. The site was the focus of long-term Archaeological investigations

(1986–99) undertaken by the Early Mines Research Group, and they uncovered what has to be the best preserved example of a British, Early Bronze Age opencast upland 'trench' mine (dating to *c.* 2000–1600 BC), along with much fascinating evidence relating to the mining that took place here during this time (Timberlake 2003).

However, although the radiocarbon dates obtained from material found at Copa Hill indicate that the main period of prehistoric mining took place here during the first two centuries of the second millennium BC, tantalising evidence has also been found at the site, which hints at an earlier Copper Age origin for the mine. The first piece of evidence in this regard is the 5-metre-long split and hollowed out alder log that was found *in situ* in a working area in front of the mine. It is likely that this object was used a drain or launder that carried away water from the deeper mine (Timberlake 2009: 109–110). A possible alternative (or additional) function for this object, is that it was used to wash hand-crushed ore, with the lighter copper ore washed further along the launder than its closely associated, but heavier, lead counterpart (Timberlake 2003: 69; 2009: 110). Perhaps the most interesting aspect of this unique artefact, however, was that it was radiocarbon dated to between 2400 and 1750 BC (Timberlake 2009:

27. Banc Tynddol Beaker grave.
(Simon Timberlake)

110), raising the possibility that it was in use during the Copper Age. Although much smaller in scale than the mining that took place in the Early Bronze Age, further evidence in the form of very small waste pits, pointing to the extraction of ore in the Early Copper Age, was also found at Copa Hill (Timberlake 2003: 115).

The wooden launder was undoubtedly an important discovery, but by far the most interesting discovery in regard to the idea that mining at Copa Hill began in the Copper Age was the small, circular disc made from thin sheet gold, which was found just below the prehistoric mine during the excavation of a Roman and early medieval lead-smelting site at Banc Tynddol (Timberlake *et al.* 2004; Timberlake 2009). This disc featured *repoussé* decoration and was centrally perforated, suggesting it had once been attached to a garment of some sort. After closer inspection of the disc by the National Museum of Wales, it was identified as an example of a 'sun-disc', items which were made by Beaker goldsmiths during the earlier centuries of the Copper Age. Similarly decorated discs have been found in Brittany, Scotland, England and Ireland, although the greatest concentration of similar discs is to be found in south-west Ireland.

The Banc Tynddol disc was discovered in the top layer of an oval, shallow-cut grave (*c.* 2m in length) that appears to have been covered by a cairn of small boulders (27); interestingly, the grave only lay about 200m from the prehistoric mine, which overlooked the site. The location of the disc in the upper half of the grave perhaps suggests that it was worn on the chest area of a garment, although we cannot be sure of this, as unfortunately only very tiny scraps of bone survived in the grave. Thus it was not possible to gain any sort of conclusive date for the burial and to discern the orientation of the deceased in the grave. It could be that the grave represents the final resting place of a Beaker immigrant, who was somehow involved in the first extraction of copper ore from this somewhat remote Welsh hillside over four thousand years ago. This is an idea that undeniably remains in the world of speculation, rather than in the concrete one of facts, but it remains an intriguing possibility, nonetheless. It should also be mentioned that the Banc Tynddol disc shows some similarities with examples found in northern England, Scotland and Brittany.

Although the evidence for Copper Age mining at Copa Hill is admittedly meagre and somewhat inconclusive, further third millennium BC radiocarbon dates obtained from the mines of Tyn y Fron and Erglodd (also in Ceridgion) lend further weight to the idea that the extraction or copper ore (whether by indigenous or immigrant groups, or a combination of the two) was a feature of life here during the Copper Age (Timberlake 2009: 104, 109 – Table 7.1). In respect of the possible identity of Wales' first copper miners we should perhaps bear in mind the possible evidence for Irish prospecting groups that was mentioned in the last chapter and also the copper halberd (these possible weapons will be discussed in more detail in the final chapter) made from similar metal to that produced at Ross Island, which was discovered near a nineteenth-century copper mine not far from Copa Hill (*ibid.*: 104).

28. Alderley Edge. (Brian Mutton)

29. Engine Vein, Alderley Edge. (Brian Mutton)

Other Evidence for Copper Age Mining in Britain

It seems somewhat unlikely that Wales stood alone as the only area of ore extraction in the British Copper Age, and there are hints to be found that perhaps lend some support this idea. For example, discoveries of stone hammers in old iron mines in the Forest of Dean may predate the Bronze (Wright in Timberlake 2009: 94) and likewise, similar tools and evidence for prehistoric mining found in the Isle of Man could be related to Copper Age mining here (Timberlake 2009: 99). A site of considerable importance in regard to ancient mining is Alderley Edge (28) in north-east Cheshire, which has yielded firm evidence that both Early Bronze Age and Roman miners dug copper ore from this beautifully wooded sandstone ridge (Timberlake & Prag 2005). Although the evidence for Copper Age mining on the Edge is far from conclusive, there were intriguing signs pointing in this direction: a radiocarbon date of *c.* 2400 BC was obtained during excavations of the Early Bronze Age pit-workings at 'Engine Vein' (29) and several flint 'thumb-nail' scrapers, reminiscent of those commonly used by Beaker groups, were also found here.

Rather surprisingly, evidence for Chalcolithic (or Early Bronze Age) mining is virtually lacking in other copper-rich areas of Britain such as Snowdonia, the Lake District and areas of southern Scotland, and the reasons for this absence remain something of a mystery (Timberlake 2009: 101). However, it seems unlikely that further discoveries relating to the prehistoric mining of copper ore in Britain will not be made at some point in the future.

Of course, as we have seen, gold artefacts were also made during the British Copper Age, and whilst some of these may have been made from imported continental gold (and perhaps also brought in as finished artefacts), it seems likely that some, if not most of the Beaker goldwork was made from alluvial gold found in streams and rivers.

Unsurprisingly, it is difficult to identify the actual sites connected with Beaker gold prospectors in Britain (Fitzpatrick 2009: 180), although analysis of the Beaker 'sun-disc' found at Copa Hill suggests that it is made from Irish gold, but this has not been conclusively proven (Timberlake 2009: 103). It is also worth noting that the lunula found near Llanllyfni in the Llŷn Peninsula, North Wales (plate 17), lies less than 20km from the Dolgellau goldfield in Snowdonia, and lunulae found in Scotland also lie fairly close to alluvial gold deposits (Timberlake 2009: 104). Furthermore, the lunulae found at Harlyn Bay and St Juliot in Cornwall contain traces of tin, suggesting that they may have been made from local alluvial gold (*ibid.*). We will look more closely at the intriguing and beautiful lunulae that were probably made by Beaker goldsmiths in Chapter Four.

Metalworking as 'Magic' in the Copper Age

One thing that should be borne in mind when considering metalworking in the Copper Age is that this process was probably viewed with a certain level of awe by those who were not privy to its secrets, and it would not be fanciful to suggest that smiths of this time were seen as something akin to sorcerers. As Paul Budd and Timothy Taylor (1995) have said in regard to prehistoric metalworking, 'the ability to put on a show of colourful, transmogrifying pyrotechnics may have commanded considerable respect' and thus the earliest copper smiths might well have been a 'political leader and magician coinciding in one single person' (*ibid.*). Bearing this theory in mind, we should perhaps turn once again to the Amesbury Archer, as among the superb array of grave-goods (which strongly hint at his high status), it will be recalled that there was a cushion stone, which many archaeologists feel were used as small anvils by Beaker smiths to produce small items of gold and copper. It may also be possible that the boars' tusks buried with the archer were used in the burnishing and smoothing of copper and gold, which are both soft metals that are easily worked (Fitzpatrick 2009: 180). Thus the Archer could have acquired his status because he had the ability to 'conjure' beautiful objects of shining metal from the ground, although Jan Turek (2004: 151) has said in regard to the idea of high-status Beaker smiths, 'it is hard to imagine that there would be highly specialised individuals dealing exclusively with metal production'. Rather, he has suggested (*ibid.*) that probable metalworking tools found in Beaker burials were symbolic artefacts that expressed the social status and prestige of an elite whose power may have been acquired through their privileged access to the exclusive new technology of metalworking.

Ritual and 'Spiritual' Aspects of Copper Age Metalwork

Just as the stone axes of Neolithic farming communities appear to have been imbued with a deeper symbolic significance that went beyond their everyday use as both tools and weapons (many were deliberately deposited in religious monuments and watery locations, probably as offerings to supernatural forces), it seems that this was the case with the earliest metal axes (plate 4). Evidence that the first metal axes were used as utilitarian tools is scarce (though this is hardly surprising), but axe marks have been discovered on the timbers of a wooden trackway (*c.* 2260 BC) that crossed a bog at Corlea in County Longford, and although dating to the Early Bronze Age (2050–2049 BC), it is evident that metal axes were used in the construction of the remarkable timber circle ('Seahenge') found at Holme-next-the-Sea in Norfolk (Pryor 2003: 266–267; Pryor 2002). That axes were also used in domestic contexts is suggested by the discovery of a copper axe fragment in a house at the Lough Gur Beaker settlement in County Limerick and several flat copper axes have also been found in the immediate locality of Lough Gur (O'Brien 2004: 566).

Although we can never fully recover the motivations behind the ritual deposition of metal axes, it is probable that they were, in some way, connected to beliefs about unknown spirits and deities. A likely example of one such votive deposit comes from Moel Arthur, which is one of the hills that form the beautiful Clwydian Range in North Wales. A hoard of copper axes was found within the walls of the later Iron Age hillfort that crowned the summit. Although it is possible that the axes were deposited here for safekeeping by someone, we would have to ask why whoever buried them did not return for what, at the time, must have been rather 'valuable' and prestigious objects, as well as why they chose this rather inaccessible location when there would have been many lower-lying locations equally suited to this task. It is in Ireland, however, that we find the most plentiful evidence pointing towards the votive deposition of early metal axes. Probable examples of such deposits include the two copper axes that were found with two rounded stones and a boar's tusk near Dunshauglin, County Meath, and the five copper axes that were found in a bog that lay between the towns of Toome and Randalstown in County Antrim (Waddell 2000: 125). Other discoveries made in Ireland indicate that it was not just copper axes that were used in votive deposits, as a copper dagger and halberd were found in 1892 along with several copper axes at an impressive depth of 10m in a bog near Birr in County Offaly, and a copper dagger was also found buried in a bog near Fivemiletown in County Tyrone (*ibid.*). Although dating to the beginning of the Early Bronze Age *c.* 2200–2000 BC, the hoard of ten or eleven axes found at Carhan in County Kerry surely provides us with a fascinating example of the ritual practice of returning metalwork back to the earth, from which it had ultimately sprung. Here, ten or eleven bronze axes had been placed in a slab-covered hollow, which lay underneath a large stone in a small river channel; the axes were arranged in a circle with their cutting edges pointing outwards and they surrounded a pile of wood ashes and small deer bone fragments that lay at their centre (*ibid.*). It is also interesting to note that none of the Irish axes have been found in association with any traces of a haft, which reveals that, at least for part of the time, they were not used as working tools and when deposited, 'were more than "axes" in the utilitarian sense of the word' (Dickins 1996: 164).

Some insights (but not truths) into the ideology surrounding the earliest metal axes (and other objects) may be gleaned from ethnographic data. For example, Jane Dickins (*ibid.*: 165) has drawn an analogy (which she readily admits is a remote one) between the Irish axes and the sacred objects or *tjurunga* (passed down by spirit ancestors) of the Central Australian aborigines, which are hidden away in isolated caves and rock shelters until a person is initiated into adulthood. In ancient West Mexico (*c.* AD 600–1521), gold and silvery objects appear to have been viewed by Tarascan peoples as divine objects associated with the sun and the moon (Hosler 1995: 105) and likewise, the Aztecs and Mexica in central Mexico associated golden and silvery colours with solar and lunar deities. It is worth mentioning that objects made from copper ore containing high levels of arsenic would have had a golden or silvery hue when finished (*ibid.*: 101) and it will be recalled that the metal ore from Ross Island was rich in arsenic. Further ethnographic evidence for the sacred significance of metal amongst non-western societies has been gathered from some Native American peoples. For instance, the *Ojibwe* people, who lived around Lake Superior in Michigan, traditionally associated copper with a supernatural being known variously as Underwater Manitou, Underwater Panther, Long-Tailed Underwater Panther, Mishebeshu or

Michi-Pichoux, the Great Lynx (Clark & Martin 2005: 118). In the nineteenth century, Keatanang, chief of the *Ontonagons* of Upper Michigan, told a white fur trader who had asked him to surrender a piece of copper:

> The lump of copper in the forest is a great treasure for me. It was so to my father and grandfather. It is our hope and our protection. Through it I have caught many beavers, killed many bears. Through its magic assistance [I] have been victorious in all my battles, and with it I have killed all our foes. Through it, too, I have always remained healthy and reached that great age in which thou now findest me.
> Kohl in Clark & Martin 2005: 120

Thus it can be seen how both archaeology and anthropology suggest that we should not lose sight of the non-utilitarian aspects of metal in Copper Age Britain and, as Mircea Eliade (in Barber 2000; 164) has eloquently said:

> The discovery of metals and the progress of metallurgy radically modified the human mode of being in the universe. Not only did the manipulation of metals contribute to man's conquest of the material world; it also changed his world of meaning. The metals opened for him a new mythological world and universe...the symbologies, mythologies, and rituals accompanying these technological discoveries played a no less important role in shaping post-Neolithic man than did the empirical discoveries themselves.

Flint Mines

Of course, while the arrival of copper mining on British shores undoubtedly marks a hugely important turning point in British prehistory (and indeed in the story of Britain as a whole), it should be borne in mind that at least some of the long-established flint mines of the Neolithic seem to have continued in use into the Copper Age, and beyond. This appears to have been the case at the justly famous Grimes Graves in Norfolk, where the black high-quality flint known as 'floorstone' continued to be mined from underground seams at least until around 2000 BC, if not a couple of centuries later, and surface deposits may have continued to be worked well into the Early Bronze Age (Prior 2003: 154; Edmonds 1995: 182). Several flint mines are also known in West Sussex and some of these have produced evidence indicating post-Neolithic exploitation in the Copper Age and Early Bronze Age (Barber 2005). For example, at Blackpatch burials featuring Beakers and Collared Urns were clearly associated with mining debris, although admittedly, this association is not clear-cut and it could be that the burials were made long after the mine had gone out of use. Nevertheless, a round barrow (Barrow 12), which overlay an earlier mine shaft, was not only cut through on its eastern side by a later mine shaft, but on the north was also covered by mining spoil and debris. Although no clearly datable artefacts were recovered from the barrow, it is quite possible that it was constructed in the Copper, or Early Bronze Age. Further suggestive evidence of post-Neolithic mining at Blackpatch was found in an area known as 'Floor 2', which appears to have been used by miners as a place where flint nodules were knapped. Here, cremated human remains and Beaker pottery were found mixed in with the flint and knapping waste and Floor 2 was probably (but not definitely) cut through by a mining shaft, and also covered by a dump of mining rubble. Perhaps the strongest indication of post-Neolithic mining at Blackpatch came from Barrow 9. The ditch was filled with a layer or 'pavement' of closely packed flint nodules which ran around its entire circuit; below this, in the southern part of the ditch, human bones, Beaker sherds and antler were found. There is a good chance that the flint layer in the ditch represents material that was taken from below ground during a period of post-Neolithic mining at Blackpatch.

Some 2km south-east from Blackpatch is the Church Hill flint mine which was thoroughly excavated by John Pull in the first half of the twentieth century. In the uppermost fill of the first shaft that he investigated he discovered sherds from Grooved Ware vessels, Beakers, Collared Urns, and possibly from Food Vessels and Peterborough Ware also. As Cecil Curwen (1954: 115) tells us, '[i]n the upper part of the filling of the shaft occurred a remarkable burial – a cremation inside a 'beaker' vessel of unusual form, accompanied by two flint axes of elongated oval form. This was covered by a layer of brown clay which in turn was overlaid by a tip of chalk blocks from a neighbouring shaft and by a flaking-floor'. Pull also found Beaker and Collared Urn sherds mixed in with mining debris in the upper fill of shaft four and noted the occurrence of Beaker sherds on a working floor, covered in mining rubble (Barber 2005: 103).

Intriguingly, as Peter Topping (2005: 81) has noted, at most English flint mines there was no real need to sink deep shafts, as adequate supplies of surface flint were often readily available. In addition to this, many of the southern English flint mines dominate the landscapes in which they are located and command spectacular views (Pryor 2005: 155). Such evidence, then, suggests that flint mines were viewed as more than just 'industrial' sites which provided abundant raw material for the production of tools and weapons, and that their location often took precedence over practicality. Although such an idea can never be proved, it does seem likely that this was because the flint mines were located in areas of the landscape that had long been seen by prehistoric communities as being somehow special (*ibid.*). Peter Topping (2005: 84) has suggested that many of the prominently sited South Downs flint mines may have been deliberately located 'in a doubly liminal zone, carefully placed between the earth and the sky, but also between the surface and the underworld'. Topping (*ibid.*) further states, '[some] flint mines were a marked focus in the cultural landscape, they were a portal between the people and the world of the spirits'. The fact that deliberate deposits of pottery, antler picks, animal and human bones, are typically found in the mines, along with unusual axe markings and miners' 'graffiti' (Pryor 2003: 155) lends considerable support to such ideas.

3

EXAMINING BEAKERS AND GROOVED WARE

It is hardly surprising that Beakers have received considerable attention from British archaeologists, as these often finely made and highly decorated vessels are distributed widely throughout Britain, and were usually linked by earlier archaeologists with invasion from the Continent (Gibson 2002: 92). I do not intend to get bogged down here in the complex issues surrounding Beaker typology and chronology, but it should be noted that it is evident that there were separate and distinct types of Beakers used in Britain, and Humphrey Case (1993) proposed four regional groups with a fifth in Ireland. Those readers who wish to more fully investigate the knotty problems of Beaker typo-chronology are directed in the first instance to: Case 1993 & 1997, Clarke 1970 & Needham 2005.

Also used alongside Beakers during the Copper Age were the equally distinctive pots made by people of the Grooved Ware culture (30 & 31). Outside of the Orkneys, Grooved Ware pottery tends to be found on ritual and ceremonial sites in Britain, and although the pots of this ceramic tradition are generally not as well made as Beakers, they nevertheless also carry their own striking and complex decoration and can be quite impressive artefacts.

In this chapter we will look at what these two separate types of pottery may reveal about their makers. Before we do so, however, it should be mentioned that Beakers and Grooved Ware were not the only types of pottery to be used by Britain's Copper Age communities. For example, in Shetland, boldly decorated pots known as Shetland Stone House Wares (32) have been found in association with thick-walled prehistoric houses, and as Alex Gibson notes (2002: 92), the radiocarbon dates obtained from these dwellings indicate that this pottery was still being made for some time after the first appearance of Beakers in the mid-third millennium BC. In the Western Isles, we have short-necked, high-shouldered vessels known as Kilellan jars, which like the Stonehouse Wares, were used alongside Beakers (ibid.). In addition to these Scottish ceramic traditions, there is the distinctive pottery used by the 'Ronaldsway culture' (33), which was confined to the Isle of Man. Radiocarbon dates obtained from carboniferous food deposits found on pottery recovered from Ronaldsway Culture sites reveal that this prehistoric Manx ceramic tradition also overlapped with that of the Beaker culture and had a long heritage spanning much of the third millennium BC (Burrow & Darvill 1997).

Beakers: Evidence of Altered States of Consciousness?

Since earlier antiquarians first started 'excavating' Beakers from the graves of their prehistoric owners, many past and present scholars have viewed them as ritual drinking vessels that held alcohol or some other mind-altering substance, and some interesting theories have been forward in this regard. Amongst these is the well-known proposal of Colin Burgess and Steven Shennan (1976) that Beakers and the other distinctive items of the Beaker 'package' spread across Europe not through the movement of people, but rather through the spread of a new and attractive religious cult, which centred on male drinking rituals and intoxication. Burgess and Shennan drew an analogy with the Peyote Cult, which was centred on the eating of the hallucinatory Peyote cactus, and which spread rapidly and extensively through the Indian tribes of North America in the late nineteenth and early twentieth centuries (Barber 1941: 673, Brodie 1994: 19). As we will briefly see in the next chapter, evidence found in the Pecos River Region, on the Texas–Mexico border, indicates that Peyote was being used as a hallucinogen long before this time. Andrew Sherratt (1987: 101) disagreed with the peyote cult analogy, but in a similar vein to Burgess and Shennan, he felt that Beakers (and the weaponry associated with them) spread throughout Europe because an emphasis on warrior feasting and hospitality emerged in the third millennium BC, and that Beakers filled with some sort of mead or beer were 'the social lubricant of this process' (*ibid.*: 93).

Following in the footsteps of Sherrat, but filling the Beakers with a somewhat less flavoursome alternative to beer, was B.G. Scott (1977: 31), who suggested that if the Beakers were indeed the central components of a cult package, they may have held the urine of people who had previously ingested the hallucinogenic toadstool, *A. Muscaria*, which is more commonly known as *fly agaric*; or some other type of drink that had been infused with these mushrooms. As Scott (*ibid.*) notes, *A. Muscaria* contains several psychoactive substances and even a moderately small number of these mushrooms could produce the desired effect. Although this idea did not find much favour amongst the archaeological community (Guerra-Doce 2006: 248), it is perhaps not as far-fetched as it might seem at first sight, as it has been plausibly argued (La Barre in Merlin 2003: 296) that humans in pre-industrial societies were 'culturally programmed' to seek out hallucinogenic plants and fungi that allowed them to communicate with the supernatural world. Likewise, as Andrew Sherratt (1995: 26) has argued, it seems likely that early human societies 'discovered the psychoactive properties of the plants in their environment, and [subsequently] canonized their usage in culturally characteristic forms of consumption and ritual'. It is also worth noting that several Siberian tribes drank *A. Muscaria* infused urine, and, '[i]t is well documented that rites involving *A. Muscaria* have included the drinking of urine from intoxicated priests (Scott 1977: 31), although, of course, such ethnographic evidence does not provide a mirror image of Beaker society.

In fact, it seems highly unlikely that the *fly agaric* toadstool, 'with its enticing bright-red, white-spotted cap' (Burl 1989: 106) escaped the attention of Beaker communities and one wonders how many people may have died as they possibly sought 'spiritual enlightenment' through *fly agaric* toadstools, as they are very dangerous and can only be eaten in small amounts (*ibid.*). Perhaps their distinctive caps served as a warning to people who would have been closer to the natural world than us, and thus they were indeed careful when they used these striking toadstools. Also, Beaker people might well have already been well aware of the dangers and hallucinogenic potential of *fly agaric*, as the use of this fungus as a mind-altering substance may have already had a long and well-established heritage in prehistoric Europe. It is perhaps also possible that hallucinogenic beverages made from the far less dangerous but equally potent (if taken in large enough quantities) Liberty Cap (*Psilocybe* spp.) 'magic mushroom' were also drunk from Beakers.

While the ideas of scholars such as Burgess and Shennan are undeniably interesting, it no longer appears tenable to accept the idea of the Beaker cult package. As we have seen, the evidence is growing that it was immigrants who initially brought the Beaker culture to Britain and not Late Neolithic communities who were unable to resist this foreign cult, which revolved around striking pots filled with intoxicating beer, or mind-bending hallucinogenic urine. Neil Brodie (1994: 19) has also argued that the peyote cult analogy is not a good one, as it represented a response by Native Americans to the dominant white culture. Indeed, to the Indians it was an alternative religion that allowed them to maintain a distance from Christianity 'and to restore ... a stable orientation, a sense of satisfaction and meaningfulness in life' (Barber 1941: 673). In any case, as will be seen below, analysis of deposits surviving within Grooved Ware pottery suggests that the Late Neolithic communities who used them were already well acquainted with beer (and perhaps also hallucinogenic beverages) and thus had no need of imported prehistoric beer or drugs from the Continent. Likewise, the evidence for immigration argues against the theories that Beakers (and their associated artefacts) appeared in Britain because they were used by competing Late Neolithic elites or 'big men' as prestige goods that could be exchanged for political support (Thorpe & Richards 1984), or as restricted status symbols which helped to reinforce their positions of power (Thomas in Brodie 1994: 14). Nevertheless, this does not mean that Late Neolithic people in Britain did not use Beakers and other Beaker items as a means of displaying their rank or status, and that native communities had no part to play in the dissemination of the Beaker Culture into Britain. As Torben Sarauw (2008: 40) has argued, 'the very distinctive Bell Beaker objects such as copper daggers, Bell Beakers, wrist guards, and barbed-and-tanged arrowheads, must have been attractive to many people because such objects had a potential in relation to the transmission of power or identity and thus carried a high symbolic value'. Perhaps of more importance to Late Neolithic communities in Britain, however, was the fact that the novel Beaker goods (in particular those made of metal) introduced by the mysterious and exotic newcomers were very different from what they were accustomed to, and as a result they had a strong desire to own similar objects (*ibid.*). In no small part, this adoption of the

Beaker 'package' probably helps to explain the subsequent rapid and widespread dispersal of the Beaker culture in Britain after its initial introduction by Beaker immigrants.

Leaving aside arguments about the introduction of the Beaker culture into Britain, it is clear that some Beakers did hold beverages that would have led to altered states of consciousness, and some of the best evidence in this respect comes from Spain (Rojo *et al.* in Guerra-Doce 2006: 249–250). For example, there is the Maritime Beaker found in one of the five undisturbed graves discovered inside the cave of Calvari d' Amposta, Tarragona (Rojo *et al.* in Guerra-Doce 2006: 249). This Beaker contained traces of beer and the alkaloid hyoscyamine, which is highly psychotropic and thus it appears that it once held a potent brew. Whoever had drunk from this pot had very probably experienced strong hallucinations and a radical alteration of his or her reality. Although, unlike the former, they did not contain a 'mind-blowing' beverage, three Maritime Beakers found in the burial mound known as Túmulo de la Sima (Miño de Medinaceli, Soria) had contained beer; also identified in another Maritime Beaker found in a badly disturbed Beaker grave, which had been dug into the barrow that covered the collective tomb of La Peña de la Abuela at Ambrona, Soria. In regard to the evidence for alcoholic beverages of some sort in British Beakers, it has to be said that this is rather scarce to say the least (although this may perhaps be partly due to the fact that there has been inadequate analysis of their contents). Our best candidate in this regard is the Beaker found in a cist grave at Ashgrove Farm in Fife (Henshall 1964). Later analysis of a deposit partly covering the floor of the grave and the skeleton found in it, identified lime tree pollen and meadowsweet, and these two species were also noted within the Beaker itself (Dickson 1978). It was concluded from this evidence (*ibid.*: 112) that the Beaker had once been filled with a mead made from lime honey flavoured with meadowsweet flowers, but that it had fallen over at some point in the distant past, spilling its contents. Although it is possible that rather than mead, the Ashgrove Beaker had actually contained honey (Brodie 1994: 19), Dickson's theory seems the more likely (Tipping in Guerra-Doce 2006: 248).

Another intriguing possibility to consider is that there may have been some connection between early All-Over-Cord Beakers and the use of cannabis, or 'hemp' as it is also known. Andrew Sherrat (1987: 97) has suggested that like the Sredny Stog culture of the Eurasian steppes, from where the tradition had initially spread west in the third millennium BC, the makers of AOC pottery also used cannabis as a social intoxicant, and likewise celebrated its use by impressing their pottery with twisted strands of this psychoactive plant. Actual evidence of the use of cannabis as a narcotic by the prehistoric inhabitants of the steppes is not wholly conclusive, but small, cord-decorated pottery vessels, which are felt to be braziers, are commonly found in graves of the catacomb-grave and pit-grave cultures. Similar vessels have been found in association with hemp seeds in third-millennium graves in Romania and the Caucasus (Sherrat 1995: 27). The famous Greek Historian, Herodotus (Book IV: 75), also provides us with what seems to be the first ethnographic account of the use of cannabis as a narcotic, although it relates to a post-funerary ritual of the later Scythians (*c.* 700 BC–AD 300) who lived around the northern shores of the Black Sea:

> Then they take some hemp seed, creep into the tent, and throw the seed on the hot stones. At once it begins to smoke, giving off a vapour unsurpassed by any vapour-bath that one could find in Greece. The Scythians enjoy it so much that they howl with pleasure.

Herodotus (*ibid.*) further tells us that, '[t]his is their substitute for an ordinary bath in water', though one suspects that in carrying out this ritual, the last thing that the Scythians had on their minds was cleaning their bodies. Although the fascinating accounts of ancient life that Herodotus has left us are rightly seen as not wholly reliable, the objects discovered in an Iron Age Scythian burial mound in the Altai Mountains confirm the validity of his account. The objects consist of the frame of a small tent in which the smoke of the hemp seeds was inhaled, a censer for burning hemp and a pot containing hemp seeds (Godwin 1967: 43, *Fig.* 1). It has to be admitted, however, that whilst it is evident that some prehistoric communities used cannabis as a narcotic, as yet, we have no evidence that the early Beaker communities who made the AOC Beakers did likewise. However, it may perhaps be interesting to note that the mysterious 'incense-cups' found in burials of the Early Bronze Age Wessex culture, which may well have grown out of the late Beaker culture, would have been very suitable for the burning of narcotics (Sherrat 1995: 28)

Other Functions of Beakers

Although the above evidence reveals that some Beakers did contain mind-altering beverages, at least on occasion, the size range of Beakers indicates they had other functions (Gibson 2002: 91); and actual confirmation of this is provided by other substances found within them. It seems likely, for instance, that some Beakers were used to hold (and cook) food, and a number of examples found in Britain appear to confirm this. Amongst these is the finely made and rather beautiful Wessex/Middle Rhine Beaker that was found along with an equally fine gold-studded bracer, a rare bone pendant and a dagger in the primary grave at the Barnack barrow in Cambridgeshire (plate 5) (Donaldson 1977), which featured several 'satellite' burials that represent at least two hundred years of funerary activity (Last 1998: 50). Inside the Beaker was a porridge-like substance, and although it has not been conclusively identified (Guerra-Doce 2006: 251), it is probable that it represents the remains of a foodstuff of some sort. It should perhaps also be noted that David Clarke (1970: 106) not unreasonably attributed Wessex/Middle Rhine Beakers to a 'rich and powerful group of settlers from the Middle Rhineland', who came mainly from the area around Mainz and Koblenz several generations after the arrival of the first Beaker settlers in Britain. Thus it is quite possible that the man buried in the Beaker grave came from this area, and his rich collection of grave goods also indicates that he was a person of some status; indeed, he could well have been an 'important local chieftain' (Donaldson 1977: 27). It is also worth noting that the greater majority of these Beakers have been found within a 60-mile radius of Stonehenge, perhaps suggesting that the renowned sacred sites of this area played a major part in attracting the 'Wessex/ Middle Rhine folk' across the Channel, or North Sea.

Another Beaker that probably once contained food was the intriguing example discovered in a cist grave at Broomend, Aberdeenshire, in the later nineteenth century (Davidson 1867). The cist contained the skeleton of an adult and child, who were buried with a large and small Beaker, respectively. Discovered within the adult's Beaker was as an antler ladle (originally interpreted as a lamp) along with '[s]mall quantities of black earthy matter [and] two or three small pieces of decayed bone' (*ibid.*: 117). It seems likely that the ladle was intended as a scoop for serving some thick gruel or soup (Shepherd in Guerra-Doce 2006: 251), or perhaps even a 'viscous honey' (Brodie 1994: 20), which both Beakers may have once contained (the child's Beaker contained the same black substance as the one associated with the adult). Also found in Scotland (at Tusculum, North Berwick) was a large AOC Beaker sherd that had 'a black, sooty incrustation still adhering to portions of the inside' (Cree 1908: 271), and it may be that this represents the remains of some type of food that the Beaker had originally contained. Presumably, those Beakers containing food (and drink), which have been found with burials, were placed in graves to provide their owners with sustenance for the journey to the afterlife. Alternatively, they may perhaps represent the remains of funerary feasts and drinking ceremonies held at the graveside by relatives or followers of the deceased. One suspects that other excavated Beakers in Britain have contained traces of food and drink, but that these have gone unnoticed, or unrecorded.

A large number of oversize Beakers or 'pot Beakers' have also been recovered from domestic sites in Britain (Gibson 1980) and David Clarke's (1970: 258) suggestion that they were used as storage jars carries some weight. Exactly what type of foodstuffs they held is unclear, but one possibility, perhaps, is that some of the largest examples held wheat and barley for making bread and beer? Wheat and milk-based products have been found in some Beakers, but these were found in Galicia (*Prieto et al.* in Prieto-Martínez 2008: 135). It could even be possible that some of these oversize Beakers were used in the preparation of mind-altering brews and functioned as drinking vessels that were passed around in communal ceremonies (Guerra-Doce 2006: 251). These may have been undertaken for religious reasons, or simply because people wished to have a drink and enjoy themselves.

Although as far as I am aware, the evidence is so far limited to sites in the Iberian Peninsula and south-western France, the discovery of Beaker sherds with copper slag encrusted on their interiors reveals that some were used as 'kilns', in which copper ore concentrates were reduced by heating, in order to produce the metal that was needed for the production of copper tools and weapons (Harrison *et al.* 1975; Guerra-Doce

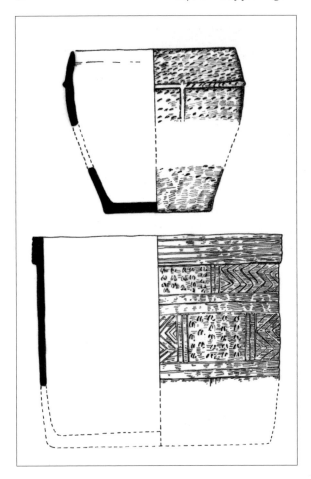

30. Grooved Ware from Durrington Walls. (Redrawn after Piggot)

31. Orkney Grooved Ware pottery. (Redrawn after Braby)

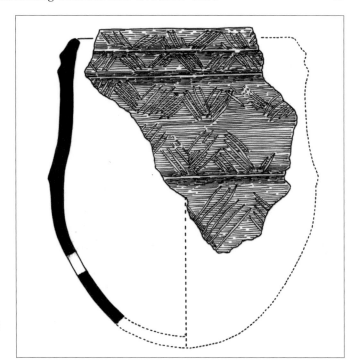

32. Shetland Stone House Ware, Ness of Gruting. (Redrawn after Calder)

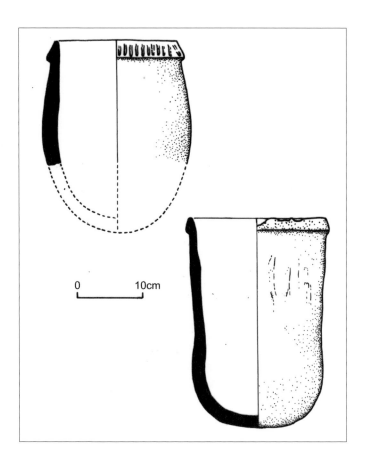

33. Ronaldsway pottery. (Redrawn after Burrow)

0   10cm

2006: 252–253; Delibes & Montero in Prieto-Martínez 2008: 135). These discoveries provide further proof that metal played an important role in Beaker society.

It is also evident the some Beakers were used to hold the remains of the dead, although this does not seem to have been common practice among British Beaker communities. One such example comes from the previously mentioned Flat Grave 119 at Radley, where the cremated remains of the two- to three-year-old (it should be pointed out that cremation of the dead was very rare among British Beaker communities) and the skeleton of the newborn baby were discovered in a Beaker that can probably be classed as belonging to Clarke's Wessex/Middle Rhine group (Barclay & Halpin 1999: 56; Cleal 1999: 204). It will also be recalled that a Beaker containing a cremation was found in the upper fill of a shaft at the Church Hill flint mines in Sussex and a Beaker deposited in a cairn at Carvinack, Cornwall, also contained a cremation (Dudley in Guerra-Doce 2006: 254).

Grooved Ware

Grooved Ware and Beakers were contemporary ceramic traditions in Britain, but unlike the latter, Grooved Ware is clearly a tradition unique to Britain (and Ireland) as it is not found on the Continent. It is also evident that this tradition was established long before the first Beaker individuals and communities from the Continent arrived on British shores. Grooved Ware was originally identified as a Neolithic ceramic tradition by Stuart Piggott in the 1930s, who later renamed it 'Rinyo-Clacton Ware' because of its widespread distribution on sites ranging from Orkney to Essex, but archaeologists have since returned to using the original 'Grooved Ware' label (Gibson 2002: 86).

As with Beakers, there are different types of Grooved Ware, and analysis of Grooved Ware pottery by Isobel Smith and Ian Longworth identified four main styles: Rinyo, Woodlands, Woodhenge (later renamed Durrington Walls) and Clacton – although the Woodlands and Clacton styles may actually represent a single tradition, rather than two separate ones (Thomas 1999: 114; Gibson 2002: 86). It may also be interesting to note that Grooved Ware pottery was never tempered with stone, unlike Peterborough Ware (contemporary with Grooved Ware until around 2500 BC, when it seems to have gone out of use) and materials such as sand and shell were used instead (Parker Pearson & Ramilisonina 1998: 855; Pryor 2003: 234). Exactly what this ceramic dichotomy represents is unclear, but it could be that 'invisible' connections were being made to the world of the dead and the living, as Peterborough Ware is often found at sites connected with the dead (e.g. caves used as sepulchres, long barrows and megalithic tombs), whilst Grooved Ware is normally recovered from ritual and ceremonial sites (e.g. henges, timber circles, pit complexes) that were frequented by large or small gatherings of people (Pryor: *ibid.*).

It is very likely that Grooved Ware developed in Orkney in the latter half of the fourth millennium BC (around 3400 BC), and subsequently spread from here, reaching southern Britain around 2800 BC (Cleal 1999: 7; Gibson 2002: 84; Harding 2003: 34; Burl 2007: 166); finally going out of use in both Scotland and England *c.* 2000 BC (Gibson 2002: 84). Exactly why it spread, however, presents archaeologists with a perplexing prehistoric puzzle that seems unlikely to ever be completely solved. However, in this respect, Aubrey Burl (2007: 166) probably hits somewhere near the mark with his suggestion that Grooved Ware pots are likely to have formed part of an attractive cult that was adopted by Late Neolithic communities in many parts of Britain. Expanding eloquently on his theory, Burl (*ibid.*: 167) says:

> Grooved Ware, tub-, barrel- and bucket-shapes were lumpish and heavy (more 'thing' than 'Ming'). Yet they are ... the everyday objects of a society converted to a new faith that cremated its dead, used the sun and the moon in its rites, possessed aesthetic objects, often of rare material, and placed dissimilar objects together, contrasting darkness and light, life and death.

Of course, we can never truly know the ethos that underpinned this cult or 'religion', which evidently bound together numerous prehistoric communities from northern Scotland to southern England for over a millennium. However, Julian Thomas (2010: 12) has recently put forward the interesting theory that Grooved Ware pottery was often connected with ritual activities and sites which 'elaborated, magnified or dramatized the idea of the domestic', and that the large social groups who were drawn together by these activities may have seen themselves as separate 'houses or households'.

Functions of Grooved Ware

Scientific examination of ancient deposits surviving within Grooved Ware pots have revealed that, like Beakers, some examples once held beer and maybe also powerful concoctions containing both alcohol and psychoactive drugs, although as we will see, as with Beakers, it is clear that this was not their only function. Inconclusive but nonetheless intriguing evidence pointing to the use of alcoholic/ narcotic beverages has been found during excavations at the remarkable Balfarg/ Balbirnie religious complex in Fife, which was in use from the Early Neolithic to the Early Bronze Age (Barclay *et al.* 1993). Analysis of burned deposits found on sherds from two very large Grooved Ware vessels, which were found in pits close to two possible wooden mortuary enclosures at Balfarg, identified – along with other macro plant remains – barley and oats. Thus it was concluded that the deposits represented the remains of 'a coarse porridge with added pottage (potherbs) and flavourings' (Moffat 1993: 109). However, it has been argued by Merryn Dineley (2004: 65) that 'it is much more likely that these are the residues from brewing, being the sediment that always settles out to the bottom of vessels used either to store or to ferment ale [and that] [t]here are striking similarities between the descriptions of the residues found at Balfarg and the appearance of barley residues that are obtained when making an ale or beer'. In addition to the evidence which probably indicates that beer was drunk by Grooved Ware groups at Balfarg, there were intriguing signs that this may have been given an 'extra kick' by the addition of Black Henbane (*Hyoscyamus niger*). Detailed analysis of a deposit encrusted on one of the sherds identified several seeds from this plant and, furthermore, these showed signs of having been deliberately crushed (*ibid.*). As has been pointed out (Cooper & Johnson in Long *et al.* 2000: 50), Henbane is poisonous, and if ingested causes euphoria, hallucinations, blurred vision, dizziness, rapid heartbeat and eventual death – if taken in large quantities. It could be then, that at Balfarg, 'the plant had a special ritual purpose [and] was used deliberately to induce intoxication, hallucinations or perhaps even death' (Dineley 2004: 67), although it should be mentioned that the deliberate use of Henbane at Balfarg has been questioned (Long *et al.* 1999; Long *et al.* 2000).

Further intriguing, but admittedly somewhat ambiguous evidence for ritual beer drinking by 'Scottish' Grooved Ware communities was found during the excavation of two stone circles on Machrie Moor, Arran (Haggarty 1991). Two timber circles that predated the monument were also discovered, and Grooved Ware sherds found in the postholes of the main circle and charcoal found in direct association with them gave dates ranging roughly from 2500–2000 BC. Although the evidence is far from conclusive 'owing to problems with Dr Moffat's computerised data' (*ibid.*: 91), it is perhaps possible that some of the residues found on the internal and external surfaces of the Grooved Ware sherds represent the remains of a honey-based mead or ale.

Prehistoric 'Breweries' on Orkney?

Merryn Dineley (2004: 41–61) has reviewed the possible evidence for the 'ritual' brewing of beer or ale at the superb stone-built settlements of the fourth and third millennium BC found on the Orkney Islands. For example, at the fascinating site of Barnhouse on Mainland Orkney (*c.* 3200–2500 BC), within the largest structure in the village (Building 8, which probably had a ritual or ceremonial function), a fairly substantial Grooved Ware Vessel was found sunk in the ground up to its rim, and analysis of residues from the pot indicate that it had originally contained barley. Therefore, it is perhaps possible that it had functioned as a 'must pot', which are used for the maintenance of a yeast culture. Several stone drains (drains are an essential feature of brewing), evidence for the removal of barley husks and clay floors that would have been suitable for 'malting' (the conversion of the starches that prohibit fermentation, into sugars) were also identified within various buildings, along with other Grooved Ware pots that may have been used as fermentation or storage vessels for malted grain, and perhaps also as containers from which beer was served. Very large *in situ* Grooved Ware pots discovered at the superb and famous site of Skara Brae (*c.* 3200–2200 BC) might have been used in a similar fashion and some of the settlement's buildings could have architectural features associated with the processing of grain into prehistoric beer(e.g. a possible kiln for drying out malted grain). While it would obviously be unwise to claim that such evidence provides proof that the Grooved Ware communities at Skara Brae, Barnhouse and other Orcadian sites were brewing and drinking prehistoric beer or ale, as Dineley (*ibid.*: 60–61) has pointed out, they did have a material culture that would have been suitable in this respect.

Grooved Ware and Elite Feasts?

Although it seems unlikely that people of the Grooved Ware culture were 'pig-pastoralists' who drove their herds from place to place in Late Neolithic Britain, as pigs are not particularly suitable animals in this respect, pig bones are often found in large quantities at Grooved Ware ritual or ceremonial sites – particularly at the Wessex henges (Harding 2003: 34). Such evidence suggests that pork feasting was part of the Grooved Ware 'complex' and that Grooved Ware vessels, which are often very large, would have been ideally suited to this purpose (*ibid.*). Scientific analysis of surviving residues on Grooved Ware pottery supports this theory. For example, that undertaken by Anna Mukherjee and her colleagues (Mukherjee *et al.* 2007) revealed that pig lipids (i.e fats, oils and waxes) were more commonly found in residues from Grooved Ware than other types of prehistoric pottery: '[r]esidues composed of predominantly porcine lipids were found in 7 per cent of Neolithic vessels (excluding Grooved Ware), 5 per cent of Bronze Age vessels and 0 per cent of Iron Age vessels; compared to 16 per cent of the Grooved Ware vessels (*ibid.*: 750). Further analysis of residues on sherds from both domestic and ceremonial sites (Mukherkjee *et al.* 2008: 2069) revealed that, with the former, only 3 per cent of the lipids could be attributed to pigs, which stood in marked contrast to the 40 per cent identified on the ceremonial sherds. However, although pigs clearly played a significant part in Grooved Ware feasts, analysis of residues on Grooved Ware sherds also indicates that not only were ruminant animals (e.g. cattle) cooked and eaten alongside pigs, but dairy products such as cheese or yogurt were also made in them (Dudd & Evershed 1999). Analysis of the Grooved Ware found at Barnhouse (Jones *et al.* 2005) revealed similar evidence and suggested that the inhabitants of this ancient Orcadian village of putative beer drinkers were not always on the 'hard stuff' and that they also drank milk, and perhaps also made dairy products from the cattle that they probably consumed.

Who actually took part in the Grooved Ware feasts remains beyond our reach, but it could be that they were restricted to a Grooved Ware elite or 'aristocracy' who sat at the head of Grooved Ware society (Bradley 1982: 35; Thorpe and Richards 1984: 77), although as Richard Bradley (*ibid.*) notes, the fact that pig bones are also found on some domestic settlements weakens this theory. Euan Mackie (1977) has compared this possible Grooved Ware elite to that of the famous Maya in central America and argued that the great Wessex henges such as Durrington Walls were the elite settlements of a 'theocratic governing class' (1997: 213), which comprised of 'wise men, magicians, astronomers, priests, poets, jurists and engineers with all their families, retainers, and attendant craftsmen and technicians' (*ibid.*: 168). As Aubrey Burl (1989: 96) has remarked, these categories may well approximate to reality if they had the words 'prehistoric' and 'non-literate' placed in front of them.

4

ART

In his book, *Image and Audience*, Richard Bradley (2009: 4) expresses his unease at the use of the term 'art' in prehistoric studies: '[t]here can be no dispassionate view of prehistoric art, because the choice of this term already makes assumptions about the past'. In other words, we are peopling the prehistoric world with 'artists' who had the same aesthetic sense and purpose as those in the Western world. I am also a little uneasy about using the term 'art' to describe the varied archaeological material covered in this chapter, but would tend to agree that 'its overlapping meanings point to representational images and to skilled craftwork, with indications of a world of symbolism: all of these are fitting' (Chippindale & Nash 2004: 22). It is also worth remembering that all of the art considered below has survived on materials that are resistant to the passage of time and it seems likely that much art has been lost because it was produced on perishable materials such as wood, textiles, and even the human body.

Rock Art

The numerous carved abstract designs that can be found on rock outcrops and boulders, and also, to a lesser degree, on ritual and funerary monuments, undoubtedly provide us with one of the most mysterious reminders of life in prehistoric Britain. The carvings are mainly confined to northern parts of Britain, with notable concentrations in southern and western Scotland and north and north-eastern England, although other groups can be found in Cumbria, Wales, Derbyshire, and the Isle of Man (Bradley 1991: 80; Sharpe *et al.* 2008: 2). For a more detailed description of the location of British rock art see Beckensall 2009. Providing a firm chronology for rock art obviously poses a problem for archaeologists, but it is evident that the majority of examples date from the Neolithic to the Early Bronze Age. In the latter period, for the most part, rock art seems to have been quarried from earlier outcrops, and perhaps also earlier monuments, and reused in funerary contexts such as cist graves and burial mounds (Bradley 1992, 2009). As Bradley (1992: 176) has said of this reuse, '[s]ymbols that may once have been directed to the wider world were turned around and directed to the dead person. Messages inscribed on a landscape that was already receding into myth were relayed exclusively to the ancestors'.

The most common and simplest motif found in the rock art repertoire is the cup-mark, which consists of small, circular depressions like inverted cones (plate 6) that were carved into rocks with hard stone tools that had pointed or chisel-like edges (Beckensall 2009: 15). An origin for cup-marks in the Neolithic is revealed by such discoveries as the cup-marked slab found in the Dalladies long barrow in north-east Scotland (Piggot 1971–72: 32, fig. 6, *ibid.*) and by their appearance in the famous Newgrange passage grave in the Boyne Valley, Ireland. Several other possible examples of Neolithic cup-marks are known, and include those found in the Llŷn Peninsula, North Wales. The capstone of the Bachwen portal dolmen (34), near the village of Clynnog Fawr, is covered in numerous cup-marks, and not far away at Cist Cerrig (an unclassifiable Neolithic tomb), on the eastern edge of the peninsula, a very curious, snake-like pattern of cup-marks can be seen on the rock outcrop that lies close to the tomb (36a & b). However, like some other putative Neolithic cup-marks, it may be that these northern Welsh examples were made in the Copper or Bronze Ages, as it is quite possible that the Bachwen and Cist Cerrig tombs continued to be venerated as sacred places by later prehistoric communities. Another Welsh example of a dolmen capstone featuring numerous cup-marks is the 'Trefael Stone', Pembrokeshire, which appears to have been moved from its original burial chamber and used as standing stone in the Early Bronze Age (*Current Archaeology* 2011). Again, the date of the cup-marks on this capstone cannot be ascertained with any certainty.

34. Bachwen portal dolmen. (Author)

While they often appear on their own, in small or random groupings on rock-faces, cup-marks not infrequently form the basic components of more complex designs and are often surrounded by one or more concentric circles (known as 'cup and ring' marks), which are sometimes breached by a radial line, or groove, running outwards from the centre of the cup like a wheel-spoke (35). Interestingly, cup-marks have also been found in close association with 'elaborated springheads' that lie close to Carn Menyn, North Pembrokeshire (Darvill & Wainwright 2011: 32), where many of the Stonehenge bluestones very probably originated. Although rare, cup-marks surrounded by square, or rectangular enclosures are also known (plate 7) and the spiral motif, which is a characteristic feature of Irish passage grave art, also occurs at a limited number of sites in Britain (Beckensall 2009: 25–30). Also uncommon are the 'penannular' (incomplete rings), 'keyhole' and 'rosette' motifs, which are sometimes combined together on rock art panels (Sharpe *et al.* 2008: 3).

Mention should perhaps also be made here of the fascinating animal carvings (probably deer) discovered at the Goatscrag rock shelter in Northumberland, which are probably prehistoric in date (37a & b). Cup-marks can also be seen just above the carvings and they are likely to date to the Early Bronze Age (or perhaps earlier), as excavations at the rock shelter have revealed that it was used as cremation cemetery by a community of this time. Although the deer carvings could be contemporary with the burials, it is perhaps possible that they have a much longer pedigree, and were made by earlier visitors to the site; could it even be possible that they were made by hunter-gatherers of the Mesolithic or Upper Palaeolithic?

35. Cup and ring marks with radial lines, Buttony, Northumberland. (Stan Beckensall)

36a and b. Cist Cerrig and
close of cup-marks on outcrop.
(Author)

37a and b. Goatscrag animal carvings, Northumberland. (Stan Beckensall)

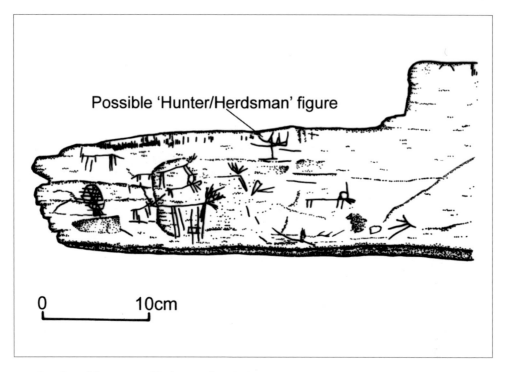

Possible 'Hunter/Herdsman' figure

0   10cm

38. Cronk yn How stone. (Redrawn after O'Connor)

In addition to the Goatscrag animal carvings, there are also those seen on the enigmatic Cronk yn How Stone from the Isle of Man (Darvill & O'Connor 2005). This slate slab was found along with another in a round barrow of uncertain date. Archaeological evidence found during excavations at the site suggests that the two slabs had originally formed a simple ceremonial structure consisting of a hearth and two flanking stones, which were roughly aligned north-west to south-east. The slab was definitely decorated on two of its faces and Face A features a collection of linear and geometric motifs. There is also a cross that was probably carved during the Early Christian phase of the site. It is Face B of the stone, however, that provides us with the most fascinating carvings, as we appear to have what are probably depictions of red deer or reindeer and perhaps also a human figure, which may represent a depiction of a hunter or herdsman (38). At the narrow end of Face B, there is a rough geometric motif filled with hatched lines. The actual date of the carving is a matter of conjecture, although it has been plausibly argued (*ibid.*: 297) that '[o]verall, the motifs represented on the Cronk yn How Stone find their closest parallels with the repertoire of designs on 3rd millennium BC artefacts and monuments in Britain and Ireland'. Thus it is possible that motifs were made in the Copper Age, although it has been suggested that it is more probable that the decoration is pre-Beaker (Tim Darvill pers. comm.), and thus dates to the Neolithic rather than the Copper Age.

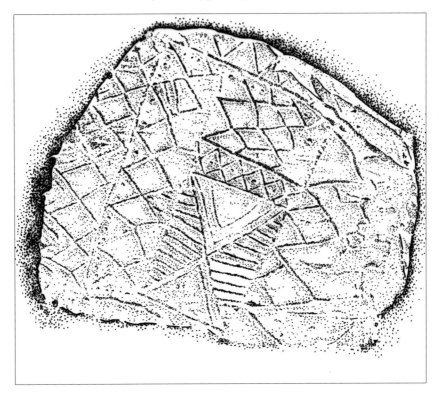

39. The Stoup Brow monument. (Author)

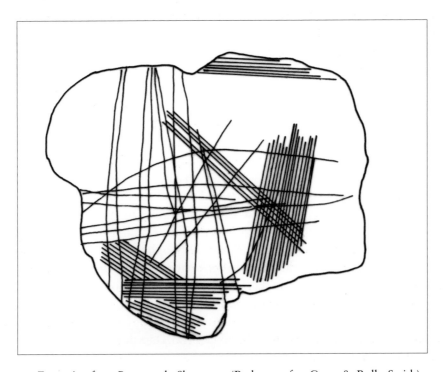

40. Engraving from Barrow 5k, Shrewton. (Redrawn after Green & Rollo-Smith)

Rock Art Speculations

As mentioned above, British rock art is a deeply mysterious phenomenon and thus we can only wander down very speculative paths in our attempts to fathom its meaning. Nevertheless, several suggestions have been put forward in this regard, with some admittedly more plausible than others and it seems fair to place that proposed by Ronald Morris (1970–71) in the latter category. He suggested (*ibid.* 55) that 'the cup-and-ring and the cup-mark may, just possibly, have been used in Europe at any rate ... as a magical aid in finding copper and gold ores, in certain well-defined positions in stone circles [and] on standing stones'. Morris (*ibid.*) further suggested that the famous rock art panel at Achnabreck (plate 8) in Kilmartin Glen (which contains Britain's largest concentration of rock art sites) may have been carved by apprentice priests or prospectors who were being taught how to make the carvings that were used as magical aids in the search for copper.

More convincingly, Andrea Arcà (2004) has argued that some of the motifs included amongst the superb Neolithic and Copper Age Alpine rock art found on Mont Bego (France) and Valcamonica (Italy) are symbolic maps or 'topographic engravings' of agricultural landscapes that were made by prehistoric communities who wished to extensively mark their territory with images, that if translated into words would say, '[t]his is my land, like my home down in the valley' (*ibid.*: 346). Richard Bradley and Ramón Fábregas Valcarce (1998: 294) have followed a similar line of reasoning in their discussion of Iberian rock art, suggesting that some of the rock art panels found next to trails may have 'acted like maps, indicating the location of different regions within the landscape and the rights that particular people may have exercised over them'.

With the idea that some rock art panels may represent prehistoric maps still in mind, an important discovery made in 2003, after a fierce fire removed large swathes of vegetation on Fylingdales Moor in North Yorkshire (Pitts 2005; Redfern 2008; Beckensall 2009), should also be noted here. Many previously unknown archaeological sites were discovered, including a number of rock art panels, and amongst these was a large stone slab that had formed part of a ring of semi-recumbent stones which edged a low cairn (now known as the 'Stoup Brow monument'). This slab features a complex and unique design (39), and Stan Beckensall believes that it is more likely that the person who produced it was inspired by Beaker decorative motifs, rather than those seen in passage grave art (pers. comm.). A second kerbstone featuring more conventional cup-marks was also found at the Stoup Brow monument. At the time of its discovery, it was suggested that the Beaker or passage grave art seen on the Stoup Brow stone could possibly be some sort of map possibly featuring a depiction of a landscape featuring mountains and sky, although this is probably unlikely. Nonetheless, although there are no convincing 'maps' found within British prehistoric rock art, it is nevertheless quite possible that some of our rock art panels were carved by prehistoric groups who wished to define, or to mark their territory.

Another unusual 'artwork' that can certainly be attributed to people of the Beaker culture was found in association with the primary burial underneath Barrow 5k, which probably represents the earliest barrow in a group of eighteen located near Shrewton in Wiltshire (Green & Rollo-Smith 1984). Excavation of Barrow 5k revealed that the primary burial consisted of a fairly deep pit cut 2.25m into the chalk, at the bottom of which lay an adult male surrounded by an unusual arrangement of very large chalk blocks (plate 9). He was buried with a fine Beaker and a copper dagger which still featured traces of the woven fabric and moss in which it had been doubly wrapped. A radiocarbon date obtained from the skeleton revealed that the burial had taken place between 2480–2200 BC (Darvill 2007: 148), placing it securely in the Copper Age. On the eastern side of the grave-pit, a small area about 30 sq. cm had been smoothed flat, and on this, someone had scratched a series of horizontal and vertical lines (40). The significance of this engraving escapes us, and perhaps it does represent nothing more than the bored doodling of someone awaiting the burial in the pit (Green & Rollo-Smith 1984: 279), but one suspects otherwise.

Alternatively – or perhaps in conjunction with its role as a territorial marker – some rock art may have marked, or made reference to, sacred areas in the landscape; places such as hills, mountains, lakes, caves and rock shelters (plates 8 & 10) that were seen as the domain of deities, ancestral spirits and other supernatural beings. Clive Waddington (1998: 35) has plausibly argued that decorated outcrops were seen as special or 'liminal places' (borders between the physical and spiritual world) in largely wooded landscapes filled with resources, and that prehistoric communities believed they could enter into a dialogue with the life-giving earth – and thus ensure it continued to provide these resources – by carving motifs into them. A suggestion also made by Waddington (*ibid.*: 46) is that the classic motif of rock art – the cup-mark surrounded by one or more rings – takes its inspiration from nature and that it mimics such things as the radiating ripples of a raindrop splashing in a puddle, the gas rings around planets and the light rings seen around stars. When we consider how bright the unpolluted night sky must have been in the prehistoric period, the suggestion that it may have inspired the standard motif of the rock-art repertoire perhaps gains some weight. However, as will be seen below, it is perhaps more likely that the sun and moon provided the inspiration for the cup and ring carvings which are ubiquitous in British rock art (although this is to not deny that some examples might be symbolic representations of the stars).

Andy Jones (2006: 217–218) has noted how many of the motifs on the decorated outcrops of the Kilmartin Valley mimic, or are framed by, the natural geological features present on the rocks such as fissures and hollows. Jones (*ibid.*: 218) suggests that this mimetic relationship thus indicates that rock surfaces were seen 'as surfaces upon which the trace of ancestral image or prior images [were] visible'. Whether they believed that ancestral or other supernatural powers actually inhabited these rocks will never be known, but interestingly, many of the motifs have 'tails' that link them to the fissures in the rock 'and appear to "enter" the rock via these cracks' (*ibid*.: 218). Is it thus perhaps possible that this linkage reveals that the people who made the rock art were trying to 'communicate', with these forces?

The people who carved the rock-art motifs would not have had the word 'shaman' in their vocabulary, but it does seem probable that they would have had ritual specialists who acted as 'agent[s] through whom contact might be established with the supernatural world' (Hadingham 1983: 92). As Aubrey Burl (1981; 149) has said: 'in a world still rabid with spirits, as ... prehistoric Britain was, shamans are likely'. Hints of the existence of prehistoric British shamans have come from burials such as that found beneath an Early Bronze Age barrow at Upton Lovell in Wiltshire, where a robust male appears to have been wearing a tunic fringed with bone points and boars' teeth when he was buried along with a female (perhaps his wife) and a varied collection of artefacts, which included a mixture of stones and pebbles (not from the locality), and five hollow nodules of iron oxide (Burl 1987: 168). Similar tunics were worn by the famous shamans or medicine men of southern Siberia (*ibid*.), although, of course, this does not prove that the Upton Lovell man held a similar role, even though the similarities are intriguing.

Whether shamans were responsible for the rock art that fascinates and frustrates us is also open to question, but evidence from the ethnographic record perhaps suggests that they were involved in its production. For example, among the Algonkian people of Canada, shamans who were on 'vision quests' would paint motifs in red ochre on rock outcrops (Arsenault 2004a: 301). An Algonkian shaman performing such a ritual act 'made the place where he stood into the exact physical centre of his experience with the sacred world, thereby linking an attainable and natural place to a distant and invisible space, the world of spirits' (*ibid*.). Much the same could be said if long-dead shamans or similar figures do indeed lie behind some of the rock art of our country. It is also perhaps possible that some British rock art panels were originally painted, as small but intriguing fragments or red ochre were found during excavations at the Hunterheugh rock-art site in Northumberland (Sharpe *et al.* 2008: 3).

If we accept that shamans or similar figures may have produced some rock art in Britain, we might also want to consider what state of mind they might have been in when they carved their motifs into its landscapes. Evan Hadingham (1983: 92) has noted that the shamans of North, South, and Central America made contact with the supernatural world through visionary experiences that were induced by hypnotic chanting or drumming, and also sometimes the use of hallucinogenic substances. Similar shamanistic practices have been noted amongst many other non-Western peoples, such as the San Bushmen of southern Africa, where shamans in trance-states are held to be responsible for the fine rock paintings found here (Lewis-Williams 1987, 1997). It has been suggested (Dobkin de Rios 1986) that the motifs in these paintings indicate that they were produced by shamans who had ingested plants with hallucinogenic properties. Even stronger pictorial evidence pointing in this direction comes from the Pecos River region, on

41. Pecos River-style rock art panel. (Redrawn after Boyd & Dering)

the Texas/Mexico border, where various caves and rock shelters feature some of
the most impressive prehistoric rock art to be found anywhere in the world (Boyd
& Dering 1996). The best represented and oldest rock art is known as the 'Pecos
River Style', which dates from *c.* 4050–2150 BC. Anthropomorphic figures seen
in the Pecos River rock paintings probably represent depictions of shamans, and
images that closely resemble *Datura* (also known as 'jimson weed', a member of
the *Solanaceae* or Nightshade family) seed pods can often be seen in association
with these (41). Among other things (e.g. delirium, disorientation), the ingestion
of *Datura* brings on hallucinations and its use by Native American shamans
seeking contact with the spirit world is well documented. For example, among the
Cahuilla Indians of California, shamans who had ingested *Datura* were required to
take magical flights to the Otherworld, where they could gain useful information
from the spirits who dwelt here. David Whitley (1992: 89) has also argued
that ethnographic data gathered on the rock art of the historic hunter-gatherer
cultures of southern California and the adjacent Great Basin region argues that
the late prehistoric/historic art found here can only have been produced either by
shamans or by initiates in ritual cults. In addition to *Datura*, depictions of what
are probably peyote buttons can also be seen alongside shamans, and actual finds
of peyote buttons from rock shelters and caves in the Pecos River region seem to
confirm the prehistoric use of this hallucinogenic cactus. Although examples are
rare (perhaps unsurprisingly) *Datura* seeds have also have been recovered from
some of these sites.

Although finding evidence of hypnotic chanting in prehistoric Britain is
obviously impossible, as will be seen below, a remarkable discovery made at

Folkton in Yorkshire perhaps hints at the existence of drums in the Copper Age. Whether 'spaced-out' shamans produced British rock art can never be proved, but as we saw in the last chapter, residues found on Beakers and perhaps also Grooved Ware reveal that their makers were not adverse to the odd alcoholic or hallucinogenic brew. It is has been argued by Jeremy Dronfield (1995: 261) 'that Irish passage tomb art has fundamental characteristics in common with arts based on endogenous visual phenomena (i.e. those produced in the eyes and brain rather than direct sight)'. Dronfield (*ibid.*: 272) makes the intriguing suggestion that that these visual phenomena were induced by migraines, the use of flickering light, and also the ingestion of the liberty cap mushroom. Although limited, Irish passage-tomb motifs are found on British rock art panels and Paul Brown (in Pitts 2005: 6) has suggested that the passage-tomb, or Beaker-inspired art found on the Fylingdales slab mentioned above may relate to 'entopic imagery generated by altered states of consciousness'. It should be noted, however, that Paul Bahn (2009) has been particularly scathing of the idea that rock art was produced by shamans who had entered altered states of reality, either through the use of drugs, or though some other method. He says (*ibid.*: 150), 'virtually every corpus of rock art, from any period or region, has had the label "shamanic" or "shamanist" slapped onto it for no good reason; and an obsession with linking rock art with so-called "entopics" and "altered states of consciousness" and "trance imagery" has been substituted for objective and original thought.'

I am not as dismissive as Bahn is of possible connections between prehistoric rock art and the use of hallucinogens by shamans or other similar figures, but there are perhaps more plausible interpretations regarding the symbolism of British rock art. One such interpretation is that the dominant circular motifs are sun or moon symbols, as the numerous alignments found at sites dating from the Neolithic to the Iron Age strongly suggest that they were seen as major prehistoric deities. Strong support for this theory is provided by monuments such as the marvellous recumbent stone-circles of Scotland, the majority of which date from *c.* 2900–2200 BC (Burl 2005: 36), and which were probably aligned on the moon in its southerly position. At several sites, cup-marks feature on the huge, horizontal recumbent stones and their hornlike flanking stones, and it is clear that the moon would have been 'framed' as it passed between the latter (Burl 1997: 36). Many standing stones also feature cup-marks and, more rarely, spirals; some of which seem to face significant solar or lunar events. For example, at the Four Stones stone 'circle' (plate 11) (it is actually an example of a 'Four Poster', which consist of four stones standing at the corners of a rectangle), which is located in the lovely Walton Basin, Powys. This impressive monument has cup-marks on the south-western stone and this faces the midwinter sunset. Four Posters probably date to *c.* 2200–1500 BC (Burl 2005: 39), but it may be possible that they have an earlier origin, as sherds from an AOC Beaker were found at the Lundin Farm Four Poster in Perth (Burl 1988: 183). However, the sherds were found with fragments from an Early Bronze Age Collared Urn (*ibid.*: 31) and thus they may have come from a pot that had been a treasured heirloom. Similarly, the impressive three-stone row at Trellech in mid-Wales was probably aligned on the midsummer sunset, as its central stone has two large cup-marks on its south-western face (plate 12). Near Drumtroddan in Wigtownshire, one of three standing stones was aligned north-east towards the midsummer sunrise and a rock-face nearby is covered in carved cup-marks and concentric circles (Burl 1981: 201). At the Croft Moraig stone circle in Perthshire, the cup-marks found on a now fallen outlying stone may possibly be lunar symbols, as it appears to have been aligned on the major southern moonset (Burl 1997: 42). In addition to the probable lunar and solar cup-marks seen on some religious monuments of the third and second millennium BC, there are also carved spirals, such as the unique one that curves around one of the stones belonging to the fine Temple Wood stone circle in the Kilmartin Valley (42 & plate 13).

It is not just standing stones that provide us with probable examples of 'astronomical' cup-marks and, for example, two of the boulders that surround a bell-barrow at Crick in Gwent bear cup-marks; the largest one features twenty-three cup-marks on its outer face, which faces the direction of the midwinter sunrise; the other bears seventeen on its upper surface and faces sunrise in early May and August (Ruggles 1999: 141). It may perhaps be of some interest to us that a cup-mark surrounded by three concentric circles was the traditional sun symbol of the Peublo Indians of the Rio Grande (Burl 1981: 86). Turning to the

42. Spiral engraving at Temple Wood stone circle. (Stan Beckensall)

less common spirals, it could be that like those drawn by the Hopi Indians of northern Arizona, they symbolised the journey from birth to death that every man has to follow (*ibid.*), although we are, of course, dipping our toes in deeply speculative waters with such theories. Although not aligned on a astronomical event, Stan Beckensall's rescue excavations at the Weetwood burial cairn in Northhumberland remarkably revealed that many of the cobbles which had formed the cairn featured cup-marks and these had been deliberately placed in the monument face-down, suggesting that their 'message' was directed towards the dead rather than the living (Beckensall Archive).

Beaker and Grooved Ware Decoration

The complex decoration that often appears on Grooved Ware and Beaker pottery can also, of course, be considered as art, although its true significance obviously lies in the hands of the prehistoric potters who made these vessels. However, an interesting idea raised by Rosamund Cleal (1999: 4) is that the lozenge lattice motif often seen on Grooved Ware could perhaps represent fishing nets, although as she readily admits, this theory is undermined by the fact that other than the Orcadian ones, there is a virtual absence of fish from Grooved Ware sites. However, as she further says (*ibid.*) in respect of this idea, 'it is perhaps frivolous, but not totally without interest that there is a lozenge pattern in some traditional fishermens' jerseys, indicating that the connection is obvious enough to have been made in the past'.

An intriguing aspect of Grooved Ware decoration that was brought to light by Colin Richards and Julian Thomas (1984) in their analysis of the hundreds of Grooved Ware sherds found at Durrington Walls (Wilts.) is that separate locations within the 'super-henge' were associated with different styles of Grooved Ware decoration. For instance, circular and spiral motifs were found in entrances, and other examples of this spiral/entrance association have been noted on pottery found at the Woodhenge timber circle near Durrington Walls and at Wyke Down henge in Dorset (Thomas 1999: 117). It seems then, that different motifs had different meanings, and thus were reserved for specific areas within monuments.

Alex Gibson (2002: 59) has also noted that some of the finer decoration seen on Grooved Ware and Beakers, and various other pots dating from the Late Neolithic to the Early Bronze Age, was made with 'complex and fine composite strings'. Thus Gibson (*ibid.*) has wondered that as similar strings are found on modern harps, pianos and guitars, is it perhaps possible that there were musicians playing stringed instruments amongst some of Britain's prehistoric communities? It is perhaps unlikely, but nonetheless it is a thought-provoking idea that should not be totally disregarded, as there have been rare but remarkable finds of prehistoric bone flutes in Britain, which reveal that music – no matter how simplistic – was not unknown. A broken example of a probable flute made from the carefully smoothed tibia of a swan or some other large bird was found with a cremation burial underneath an Early Bronze barrow near Stonehenge by William Cunnington, in 1808 (Megaw: 1960: 9; Burl 1987: 166). Aubrey Burl (*ibid.*) has evocatively imagined the owner of this flute 'piping to his flock during the lazy hours of a Wessex summer'. Another broken example of a probable bone flute was found with a secondary adult burial discovered by Dean Mereweather (another nineteenth-century antiquarian) in a low barrow near Avebury.

We can once again turn to the ethnographic record in our attempts to gain possible insights into the distinctive and elaborate decoration that often appears on Beakers and Grooved Ware. Of course, it is undoubtedly dangerous to assume that a one-to-one relationship exists between cultures that are separated by vast distances of time and space and we must always be aware that ethnographic analogy only offers us possibilities, rather than certainties. However, evidence from the ethnographic record does suggest that there may be more to Beaker and Grooved Ware decoration than meets the eye. Among Eton groups in northern Cameroon, for example, each motif on a decorated pot has a name and decorated pots cannot be claimed by demons for their own use, in contrast to undecorated examples (Gosselain 1992: 574). Further evidence from northern Cameroon may also lend support to the idea that Grooved Ware and Beaker decoration had deeper meanings. Judy Sterner's (1989) fascinating analysis of the pottery used by the Sirak Bulahay of the Mandara Highlands revealed that they use at least twenty-one sacred pots and these are more highly decorated than domestic ones. One of the main uses of these pots was to act as receptacles for the souls of ancestors or deceased relatives, and another of their main functions was to contain and protect against powerful and potentially dangerous spirits. Examples of these include tree or rock spirits that may have been offended by agricultural activities and the spirit associated with millet, which is the staple grain of the Sirak Bulahay. Decorated sacred pots are also made to prevent the reoccurrence of illness, and for the unfortunate victims of lighting strikes. It has also been suggested (David *et al.* 1988) that some of the decoration seen on pots made by the Bulahay and Mafa (another group from northern Cameroon) mimics specific bodily ornaments worn by members of these groups and that like these ornaments, the decoration on the pots serves a protective function against the dangerous powers that are inherent in certain individuals (e.g. sorcerers and witches), nature (e.g. mountain and rainbow sprits), and in particular, *Zhikile*, the creator god.

Ann Woodward (2008: 83) has made the intriguing suggestion that the bones, twigs, reeds and straws, which were sometimes used to decorate prehistoric pottery such as Beakers and Grooved Ware, 'may have been gathered in the wild and thus symbolised particular places or ecological zones known to the users and makers'. If bird bones were used to decorate pots, those belonging to the blackbird, magpie, crow, rook, sparrow, and jay were preferred, and thus it perhaps possible as Woodward (*ibid.*: 84) further suggests, 'that such species were regarded as possessing magical or spiritual powers, and that such power could be transferred to the pottery vessels'.

Mention should also be made here of a recent study of fifty-four Beakers from burials in Aberdeenshire, which has revealed that over half of these vessels had been enhanced with a white paste made from cremated bone (Curtis 2010: 1). Whether this paste was made from animal or human bone is not clear, but the fact that it was used in the funerary sphere does suggest that it had some symbolic significance (*ibid.*: 2).

Portable Art

As well as producing weird and wonderful abstract rock art (at least to us), Britain's Copper Age communities also produced portable or 'mobiliary' artworks and these are equally – if not more – mysterious than their larger, earthbound counterparts. It seems appropriate to begin this section with the Folkton Drums, which, it would be fair to say, provide us with a remarkable testimony to the skills of British prehistoric artisans.

The Folkton Drums

Like several nineteenth-century men of the church, the Revd William Greenwell (librarian to the Dean and Chapter of Durham Cathedral) had a keen interest in the new and burgeoning discipline of archaeology. Unfortunately, as with many other nineteenth-century antiquarians, his excavation methods left a lot to be desired and as Aubrey Burl (1981: 2) tells us, 'he contrived to dig into some three hundred barrows, gouging them in a way that has caused some archaeologists to wish that the hours he spent on his knees had been in prayer rather than in trowelling'. Nevertheless, underneath a lone barrow enclosed by two circular ditches on Folkton Wold he did discover three beautifully decorated stone cylinders or 'drums' (plate 14), which undoubtedly rank amongst the finest and most mysterious objects to have survived from prehistoric Britain. They had been placed behind the head of a five-year old girl, who had been buried in an oval pit with her hands covering her face, which looked westward (*ibid.* 4–5). The drums are made from chalk found in the locality (perhaps the nearby cliffs), with the largest having a diameter of 146 mm; the smallest 104 mm and the intermediate-sized drum 125 mm in diameter (Middleton 2004 *et al.* 3004). Although no closely dateable grave goods were found with the girl, the remnants of a smashed Beaker dating to *c.* 2300 BC were found in association with the disturbed remains of a man and woman (whose skulls were missing) buried underneath a cairn in the central burial area (Burl 1981: 3).

Ian Longworth (1999) has analysed the beautiful decoration on the drums and he suggests that the artist/s who made the drums drew heavily on motifs used on Grooved Ware pottery and Andrew Middleton *et al.* (2004) agree, as they have argued that 'the strongest resemblances taking the drums as a whole are to the decoration found on … Grooved Ware pottery'. Phillip Harding (1998: 325–326), however, feels that the decoration seen on the drums is more typical of that found on some Beakers, and this argument is worth bearing in mind, particularly when the burial context of the drums is taken into account. Perhaps though, it is more likely that rather than employing a distinct Beaker or Grooved Ware style for the drums, whoever made them instead 'drew upon a pool of motifs current at the time, *c.* 2500–2000 BC' (Middleton *et al.* 2004). Longworth (1999: 86) also notes a number of other interesting parallels seen on the drums. For example, eyebrow-and-eye motifs, or 'faces', similar to those seen on the drums, can be found on stones incorporated into the Knowth passage grave (Boyne Valley) and the Holm of Papa Westray cairn on Orkney. It is quite possible that these fascinating faces symbolise a deity of some kind who watched over the dead, or perhaps even 'deities', as the three drums are of different sizes, which perhaps indicates a triad of guardian sprits? It has also been noted (Varndell 1999: 354), that the lozenge motif, which has 'curious antennae sprouting from the top', is echoed in the decoration seen on the well-known Grooved Ware sherd recovered from Skara Brae by Gordon Childe. The opposed spiral motifs seen on top of the drums are quite closely paralleled at Barclodiad y Gawres passage grave on Anglesey, at the Pierowall and Eday Manse chambered cairns on Orkney, and on the Calderstones in Liverpool. Opposed spiral motifs can also be observed on smaller artefacts such as the finely decorated macehead found at Knowth and on Grooved Ware recovered from Pit 3196 at the Barrow Hills prehistoric religious complex (see Barclay & Halpin 1999: 80, *Fig. 4.33*).

I have the good fortune to live close to the Calderstones and a walk of ten minutes or so will bring me to its six surviving stones that now stand somewhat sadly neglected, but protected, underneath a rather dilapidated conservatory in the pleasant surroundings of Calderstones Park (43). Unfortunately they are closed to the public at present, as the dreaded 'Health & Safety' have deemed the conservatory unsafe to enter. Although the passage grave from which they originally came has long since gone, the Calderstones nevertheless provide us with fascinating and unique examples of prehistoric art (see Forde-Johnston 1957 for a detailed discussion on the stones). In addition to the opposed spirals, concentric circles, cup-marks and other prehistoric motifs seen on the Calderstones – some of which were clearly made long after the prehistoric examples – there are also rare and mysterious foot-carvings, which we could speculate may perhaps be somehow symbolic of the journey from life to death. Although we cannot say for sure when these foot-carvings were made, Paul Nash (2006: 227) feels that along with an axe, cup-marks, arcs, and a wheel motif also seen on the stones, they probably date to *c.* 2500–1800 BC. Aubrey Burl (1981: 172) has speculated that the foot-carvings could have been made by '[t]raders from the east, even from across the North Sea, [who] may have passed this way in the Early Bronze Age'. The possible carving of what may be a halberd can also be seen on one of the stones, and its shape perhaps suggests that it is of Irish type (Forde-Johnston 1957: 38). A little more will be said of halberds in the final chapter, but for now, it can be noted that these copper or bronze implements date from *c.* 2300–1900 BC (O' Flaherty 2006: 423). Intriguingly, an impressive standing stone ('Robin Hood's Stone) bearing deep vertical groves and three cup-marks at its base can also be found about a mile from the Calderstones, looking somewhat incongruous in its busy urban setting (44). Although it cannot be proved, it is quite possible that it was also once part of the Calderstones passage grave. Local folklore has it that the deep groves in the stone were caused by archers in the time of Henry VIII, who used it to sharpen their arrows, but it seems more likely that these deep striations are a natural feature.

Engraved Chalk and Stone Plaques

As Phillip Harding (1988: 325) has pointed out, with the exception of the Folkton Drums, the chalk plaques (45 & plate 15) found on King Barrow Ridge near Stonehenge provide us with the 'finest examples of engraved art on chalk'. They first came to light in the latter half of the last century, when improvements being carried out on the A303 road uncovered a pit, which along with the plaques also contained numerous sherds of Grooved Ware, various animal bones and part of an antler pick (Vacher 1969). It is hard to find exact parallels for the decoration seen on the plaques, but Harding (1988: 326) has argued that the lozenge motifs seen on the smaller plaque are commonly found on Beakers, but rarely seen on Grooved Ware. The 'Greek key' design is undoubtedly rare and the only other known example is the one seen on a Grooved Ware sherd found at the Marden Henge monument in Wiltshire (*ibid*.). It is difficult to pin down a firm date for the plaques, but calibration of initial radiocarbon dates obtained on a cattle bone and the antler found in the pit indicate that it may be more probable that they date to the Late Neolithic rather than the Copper Age (Hedges *et al.* 1993: 312; Lawson 1993: 185; Darvill 2007: 203).

Also from Wessex, there is a broken chalk plaque (46) that was discovered in 1990 by Wessex Archaeology who were carrying out excavations in advance of house building on Butterfield Down (Lawson 1993). Although the plaque was found in the upper fill of a ditch forming part of a Romano-British settlement, it probably came from the prehistoric cemetery that preceded this site and Andrew Lawson (*ibid*.: 184) feels that 'it compares most favourably' with the two plaques mentioned above. Furthermore, Lawson (*ibid*.: 185) argues that like the smaller plaque from King Barrow Ridge, the design seen on the Butterfield Down example '[finds] parallels more easily in Beaker pottery than Grooved Ware'. Several pits containing worked flint and pottery were also found nearby and in Pit 2 there was a complete and exceptionally large Beaker (Darvill 2007: 203).

Moving north from Wessex to North Yorkshire, there is the large decorated chalk plaque that was discovered in a ditch at the Romano-British site at Kilham, Hanging Cliff (Varndell 1999). The irregularly shaped slab features engravings on both faces (47), although one reveals a lot more care and skill than the other, which perhaps shows that more than one prehistoric hand was responsible for the decoration? Gillian Varndell (*ibid*.: 353) has said of this intriguing reminder of prehistoric life, '[t]he remarkable feature of the Kilham Plaque is the resemblance of its decoration to that on some Grooved Ware pottery, especially to certain internally decorated bowls'. As Varndell (*ibid*.: 354–355) further remarks,

43. The Calderstones. (Author)

44. 'Robin Hood's Stone', near
the Calderstones. (Author)

although we will never be able to grasp the true meaning of engraved plaques, the shape of the Kilham example is distinctive and this could have been of some significance to its maker; the decoration seen on the finely decorated face appears to respect this shape and to have a focal point exactly halfway along the upper edge of the plaque. When the plaque was made is unclear, although either a Late Neolithic or Copper Age date seems highly likely.

Another example of a decorated plaque is the unique and important example recently discovered at Rothley, Leicestershire (Cooper & Hunt 2005). The plaque is made from sandstone and measures about 20mm by 135mm in size, and although incomplete, it is still possible to see what very probably represents a stylised face formed by two double rings and lozenges, which is surrounded by a rectangular frame (plate 16). As has been pointed out (*ibid.*: 15), none of the decorated plaques so far discovered feature figurative art, and the closest parallel that we have for the Rothley example are the Folkton drums, which as we have seen, also display stylised faces. The plaque was found along with stone tools and thousands of Grooved Ware sherds in a flat-based pit that may represent the remains of a former building.

A decorated plaque has also been recently discovered at King's Stanley in Gloucestershire, near the foot of the Cotswold scarp (Evans 2006; 2010). The plaque is probably made from local limestone and was found in the larger of two pits that had been dug into a gravel terrace between two tributaries of the River Frome. Although the plaque is rather small (39mm by 23mm by 7mm), it is almost complete and is quite finely decorated on one side with many closely spaced inscribed lines that have been arranged in a radial or cross-like pattern (48). In addition to the plaque, a probable cylindrical bead made from a coal-like concretion (49) and, unusually, a broken sandstone bracer (measuring 60mm by 30mm by 5mm) with rounded corners and a drilled hole were also found in the pit (50). Numerous pottery sherds from at least five Grooved Ware vessels and a Mortlake pot (a sub-style of the Peterborough Ware tradition – 51) were also recovered from the pit, along with many flint tools and fragments of animal bone. A radiocarbon date obtained on hazelnut fragments suggested that the pit had had been dug in the Copper Age between 2470 and 2200 BC, which lends support to the idea that 'the Mortlake vessel was a valued special item of considerable age' (Evans 2006: 4), as the Mortlake tradition appears to have died out around 2700 BC (Gibson 2002: 82). That people buried 'heirlooms' in prehistory seems likely, and Ann Woodward (2002) has looked at the question of heirloom deposition in the Early Bronze Age and how fragments of earlier Beakers seem to have been employed as such at various sites dating to this period.

Decorated stone plaques bearing similar decoration to each other, and to that seen on the Skaill knives mentioned below, have been found at the Graig Lwyd Neolithic axe factory on the north Welsh coast above Penmaenmawr (Warren 1921: 194; Piggott 1954: 289–290), and at the prehistoric 'house' (it may have been a building that had a religious function) discovered at Ronaldsway Bay on the Isle of Man (52) (Bruce & Megaw 1947). Another decorated slate plaque, also of Manx provenance, was the one discovered at the site of Ballavarry (Burrow 1997: 38).

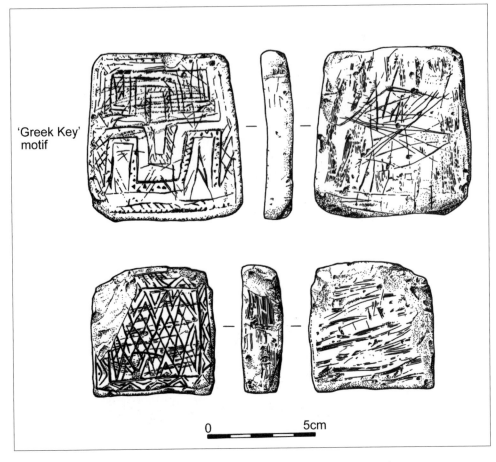

'Greek Key' motif

45. Decorated chalk plaques found near Stonehenge. (Redrawn after Harding)

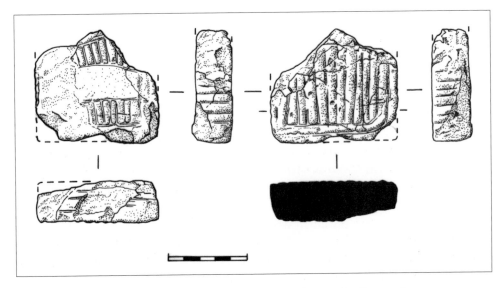

46. Decorated chalk plaque from Butterfield Down. (Redrawn after Lawson)

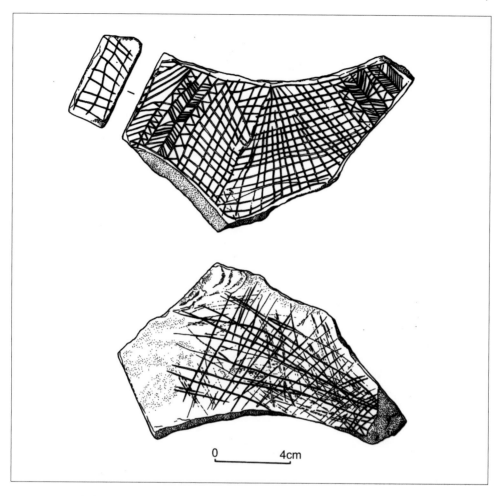

47. Decorated chalk plaque from Hanging Cliff. (Redrawn after Dean)

The date of the Graig Lwyd plaque is unclear, although it could have been left by a Copper Age 'quarryman' rather than a Neolithic one. As has previously been seen, some of the flint mines that originated in the Neolithic continued to be worked for a considerable length time after the first arrival of metal in Britain, and it seems unlikely that Neolithic axe factories came to a sudden and dramatic end; although it cannot have been that long before the stone axes that are so characteristic of the Neolithic went out of use (Edmonds 1995: 181–182). However, it should be pointed out that the prehistoric quarrying at Graig Lwyd has been dated from the final Mesolithic to the Late Neolithic *c.* 4350–2900 BC (Peterson in Price 2007: 86), so the above suggestion seems unlikely.

Bronwen Price (2007: 97), however, has made the interesting suggestion that from the Mesolithic to the Early Bronze Age, Graig Lwyd (53) 'was a focus of religious pilgrimage'. She has suggested (*ibid.*: 98) that by the Late Neolithic, 'pilgrimages to the site were explicitly initiatory in nature [and that] [t]he maturation to adulthood was facilitated through both the admission to this

48. Decorated limestone
plaque from King's
Stanley. (David Evans)

49. Bead from King's
Stanley. (David Evans)

50. Broken bracer from King's Stanley. (David Evans)

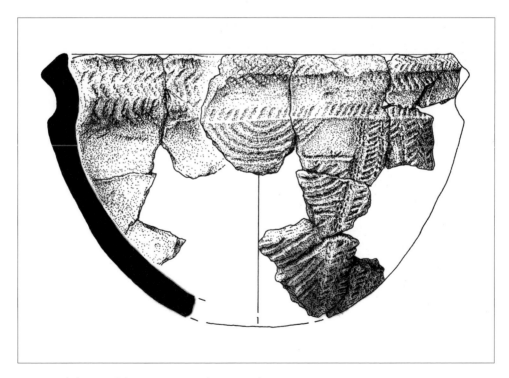

51. Mortlake vessel from King's Stanley. (David Evans)

sacred place and the revealing of the secrets of axe manufacture'. It is certainly an idea worthy of consideration, as it is evident that Neolithic axe factories in general were located in high and remote places, even though suitable stone sources could often be found below them. This indicates that these places were perceived as being special in some way and it seems likely that they were probably connected to beliefs about deities and spirits. Could it be, then, that that the Graig Lwyd plaque represents an offering left to these supernatural powers by a later prehistoric 'pilgrim' who had trekked many miles from his/her home community to this high and lonely headland on the north Welsh coast? Maybe, but it has to be admitted that such an idea is purely speculative.

It is worth mentioning that below Graig Lwyd there is a superb collection of ritual and ceremonial monuments forming a religious complex or sanctuary, which was in use from the Late Neolithic to the Early Bronze Age. The Druids' Circle (54) is the most famous of these monuments and the archaeological evidence found at this impressive and atmospheric stone circle suggests that it was probably built around 2900 BC, and that it was still being used as a sacred site over a thousand years later. The Druids' Circle is just one of the many stone circles that can be found throughout Britian, and as Aubrey Burl (2005: 29) tells us, '[t]he time when metallurgy began in Britain and Ireland and when the descendants of continental Beaker people were mixing with native people was also the time when many of the most perfect rings were built'. Thus many of Britain's finest stone circles would have been erected by Copper Age communities.

The Ronaldsway slate plaques were found in association with pottery that has been dated by carbonaceous deposits still adhering to its inner walls, and the dates indicate that the pots were made in the early centuries of the Copper Age (Burrow & Darvill 1997: 416, Figure 2). The plaque from Ballavarry was found amongst the large amounts of pottery and flint tools that were deposited in three interconnecting pits, which also featured large concentrations of charcoal (Burrow 1997: 38). Radiocarbon dates obtained from carbonaceous deposits on the pottery suggest that the pits at Balavarry also date to the latter half of the third millennium BC (Burrow & Darvill 1997: 416, Figure 2).

Decorated Stone Knives

While we cannot be completely certain as to their exact function, it is likely that the Skaill knives found in the prehistoric settlements of the Orkney and Shetland Islands were mainly used as butchering tools, although they may also have been employed as general cutting implements (Savile 1994: 104). A decorated example of a Skaill knife dating to around 2400 BC was found in one of the houses at Skara Brae (55) during excavations in the later twentieth century and features a design incorporating triangular and lozenge-shaped motifs. Similar motifs can also be seen in the many other carvings that mostly appear on the walls of the passages which linked the houses of the Skara Brae settlement. Alan Saville (*ibid.*: 110) has noted that these motifs are similar to those found on Orkney Grooved Ware pottery and thus wonders, '[c]ould the decoration on the Skara Brae knife

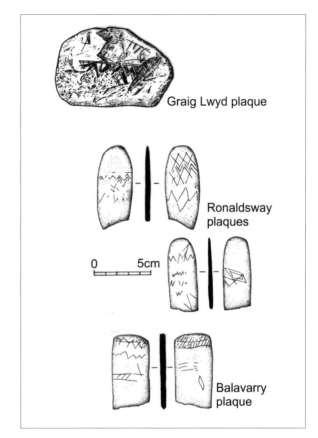

Graig Lwyd plaque

Ronaldsway plaques

0   5cm

Balavarry plaque

Right: 52. Decorated stone plaques from Graig Lwyd and the Isle of Man. (Redrawn after Piggott & Burrow)

Below: 53. Graig Lwyd seen from Monument 280, Cefn Coch. (Author)

54. Druids' Circle. (Author)

be the casual sketch or trial piece of a potter, using the convenient surface of an already discarded knife in the same way as a modern craft potter might use the back of an envelope?'

A 'discoidal' stone knife featuring similar lozenge motifs to that seen on the above was also found at Skara Brae by Gordon Childe during his famous excavations at the site in the earlier twentieth century, and the smoothness of this knife coupled with its decoration may indicate that it was a prized possession that had been repeatedly handled by its owner (*ibid.*: 108). An oval-shaped stone decorated (on all four sides) in the same fashion as the knives, was also discovered in an unknown context on Orkney, probably in the neighbourhood of Skaill (Callander 1931: 97). Some of the stone slabs used to construct the houses at Skara Brae (e.g. House 8) also feature the lozenges, chevrons, and triangles that are seen on the stone knives and elsewhere.

Although not an example of portable art as such, another interesting prehistoric 'artwork' is the decorated side-slab from a former cist grave (which would have been Copper or Early Bronze Age in date) that was found on Badden Farm in Argyll (Campbell, Scott & Piggott 1960–61). This featured a pattern of quite finely executed interlocking lozenges, and provides us with further proof of the mysterious importance of the lozenge motif to British prehistoric societies, which could be said to have reached its apogee with the superbly decorated sheet gold lozenges that were founds in the famous Bush Barrow burial.

Carved Stone Balls

These deeply enigmatic objects (56) are primarily confined to Scotland and whilst we cannot date them precisely, the motifs seen on the decorated examples, and the archaeological contexts in which they have been found, reveal that many must date from the Late Neolithic to the Early Bronze Age (Marshall 1976–77). Although a great air of mystery surrounds carved stone balls, this has not deterred scholars from proffering suggestions as to their possible function. T. N. Todd (2006: 73), for example, has proposed that their generally uniform weight, shape, and size, indicates that they were hunting weapons, 'well suited for killing birds and small animals, or deterring predators such as wolves and eagles from attacking domestic flocks, in locations where the balls would neither be damaged or lost … such as cultivated fields'. It is a plausible idea, but we may wonder why some of balls were elaborately and beautifully decorated if they were indeed used in this way (e.g. the famous example found at Towie), while others were not. However, Todd (*ibid.*: 71), has further suggested that this may be because their owners wished to identify them amongst other balls that were being used in some sort of prehistoric competition. The antiquarian, John Alexander Smith, had earlier suggested (1874–76) that the carved stone balls were weapons, although rather than being hunting weapons, he felt that they were maceheads similar to those that can be seen on the famous Bayeux Tapestry and that they had been left behind after Saxon incursions into Scotland. Clearly,

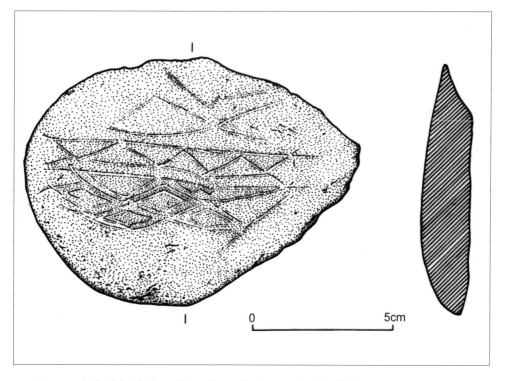

55. Decorated Skaill knife from Skara Brae. (Redrawn after Saville)

Smith was thousands of years adrift in his dating of carved stone balls and he was also well wide of the mark as regards their function because, as Dorothy Marshall (1976–77: 63) points out, 'it would be well-nigh impossible to fix the balls to a stick firmly enough for them to be used as weapons'. Writing in the early twentieth century, Ludocvic Mann (1913–14: 413) also disputed Smith's theory, but his alternative hypothesis (*ibid.*: 414) 'that they were moveable poises on primitive weighing machines' seems equally unlikely.

Other suggested possible functions of the balls are that they were used as oracles from which the future was divined, or that they were prestige or ritual objects owned by families or clans (*ibid.*: 63–64). As Mark Edmonds (1992: 185) has pointed out, it has also been proposed that certain balls 'reflect an attempt by the manufacturers to realise the five Platonic solids (i.e. the tetrahedron, cube, octahedron, dodecahedron and icosahedron)', or that 'they embodied ideas associated with the movement of the stars and the passing of the seasons' (for a discussion of the idea that the makers of carved stone balls had anticipated Plato by thousands of years, see Young 2008). Ultimately, we will never be able to discover what carved stone balls were used for or what the decoration seen on them signifies. Nevertheless, we can appreciate the highly skilled and patient craftsmanship that lies behind many examples, and it is this that provides the strongest link between us and their long-dead makers.

Beaker Goldwork

Brief mention has been made of Beaker goldwork in previous chapters, but we should examine these fragile but rather beautiful objects that were made by Beaker smiths in a little more detail. As has been pointed out (Taylor 1985: 183), these objects 'were not simply art or ornamentation but probably designated both the high social rank of a person and their political, religious or occupational status'. It should also be pointed out that less ostentatious items of Beaker 'jewellery'

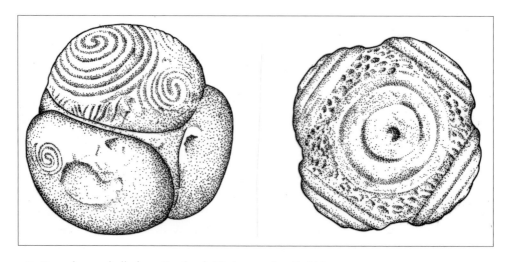

56. Carved stone balls from Scotland. (Redrawn after Smith)

have been recovered from Beaker graves. Included among these items are the bone finger rings that have been found in Beaker graves such as the one discovered at Mainsriddle, Kirkcudbrightshire (Stevenson 1956–57). The ring lay among the fingerbones of the left hand of a well-built man, aged around thirty, who was buried in cist grave with a Beaker, and was made from either bone or an antler. Similar rings have been recovered from Beaker graves discovered in the nineteenth century at Broomend of Critchie, and Clintery in Aberdeenshire (*ibid.*). It will also be recalled that bone pendants or toggles were found with the Boscombe Bowmen and the high-ranking individual laid to rest in the Barnack Beaker grave.

Returning to our brief foray into Beaker goldwork, we will begin with the lunulae (so-called because they are shaped like a crescent moon), which, without question, represent the greatest achievements of the Beaker goldsmiths. Joan Taylor's (1970) important re-analysis of these beautiful sheet-gold collars (which have their greatest concentration in north-western Ireland) identified them as being the product of Beaker artisans working in the Late Copper and Early Bronze Age (*c.* 2250–2000 BC), although not all scholars (e.g. Burl 1987: 156–157) assign them to the Beaker culture. On the basis of shape, ornamentation and geographical distribution, Taylor classified the lunulae into three groupings: Classical, Unaccomplished and Provincial, with the first two being of Irish manufacture and the third appearing to be made in western Britain, in regions along the Atlantic Seaboard. As their names imply, the Classical lunulae are distinguished by the sophistication displayed in both their manufacture and decoration, whilst the 'Unaccomplished' examples are more crudely decorated, and they also contain less gold. The Provincial lunulae (plate 17) feature more gold than the other two types (and thus are thicker), and although they are more sparsely decorated, they are nevertheless well made. Taylor (1994: 44) has plausibly argued that '[a]ll lunulae attempt to follow the rigid symmetry laws of the Beaker art-style, employing the Pan-European library of motifs' that was used by Beaker populations throughout Europe.

As to the actual function of the lunulae, it has to be admitted that we are somewhat in the dark. However, it seems unlikely that they were made as personal items, as only two from some one hundred found in Britain, Ireland, and Atlantic Europe, have been tentatively identified as possible grave goods, and rather, many have been discovered as stray finds in bogs, fields, on high ground, or buried under standing stones (Taylor 1970: 43). It is likely then, that lunulae 'performed a communal role such as emblems that signified the lineage of a chieftain (making them property of the tribe), or possibly they indicated the status of a priest (therefore, property of the temple) or perhaps the ornament of an inanimate object such as an idol (again, property of the religious sector of society)' (Taylor 1994: 42). While some lunulae may well have been buried for later retrieval (Taylor 1970: 43), it also seems possible that some were deposited as offerings to the deities and spirits that were worshipped by Beaker communities. Whatever the truth is behind the deposition (loss appears very unlikely) of lunulae, the fact that they show little sign of wear does suggest they were items that were reserved for a special purpose.

As has been previously seen, small sheet-gold basket earrings or hair tresses have been found in a limited number of early Beaker burials, with the Amesbury Archer providing the best-known example. As Andrew Sherrat (1986: 61) has noted, it was Gordon Chile who first defined these objects as basket-earrings, comparing them with the famous ear ornaments found at Troy. However, in regard to the idea that these delicately beautiful artefacts were worn as earrings by select members of Beaker society, Sherrat (*ibid.*) has said, '[t]he form of the objects, with a thin, sheet-gold "tail" wrapped around the semi-cylindrical body of the ornament, seems singularly inappropriate for attachment to an ear, even if skilfully pierced'. Perhaps then, it is more likely that these artefacts functioned as hair tresses, and as Sherrat (*ibid.*: 65) further says, '[a]fter all, the image of a figure with gold-wrapped dreadlocks is no more bizarre than that of the Varna chieftain [found with an exceptional and abundant collection of grave goods in a fifth millennium BC cemetery located on the Black Sea Coast of Bulgaria], with his gold penis sheath'. However, two pairs of these small, gold ornaments found in a richly furnished early Beaker grave at Chilbolton, Hampshire (Russel 1990) may suggest that the traditional interpretation of their function is correct. Andrew Russel (*ibid.*: 166) tells us, 'the microscopic examination of the Chilbolton finds suggests, both by the lack of wear inside the baskets and by the 5mm lengths of the unbraided tangs, that these ornaments were indeed worn in people's ears. The earring would have encased the edge of the ear, and if two pairs were worn then the ear would have a golden rim'. Whatever interpretation we favour, it is interesting to note that the larger pair of earrings/hair tresses found at Chilbolton are very similar to the pair found in the Radley Beaker grave (plate 1) and it is quite possible that both pairs were made by a single workshop or goldsmith (*ibid.*). A unique sheet-gold tubular bead was also found with the primary burial at Chilbolton (a second Beaker burial was placed in the grave shortly after the first – both burials were of adult males) and the traces of dark-brown material observed on its inner surface may indicate that it perhaps formed the centrepiece of a necklace, which primarily consisted of the small stone beads that were also found with the grave's first occupant.

We have also previously come across the small and delicate sheet-gold Beaker 'sun-discs', and as mentioned they are found in Ireland, Britain and Brittany, although it is in Ireland that the majority have been discovered. Often, the discs are embossed with circular patterns around a central cross and it is quite possible that they provide us with evidence of the veneration of a solar deity by Beaker communities, as the cross-within- the-wheel motif was an important solar symbol employed by other prehistoric societies such as the famous Celts and, interestingly, gold sun-discs similar to the Beaker discs were worn by members of the Aztec aristocracy. Joan Taylor (1994: 44) has suggested that the motifs seen on the Beaker discs were derived from the racquet-headed pins of Central Europe and were then 'refluxed' back into the Atlantic coastal area of Europe. The fact that the discs are often perforated centrally, or around their outer edges reveals that they were worn on tunics or other garments. It has also been noted by Taylor (*ibid.*: 46) that the

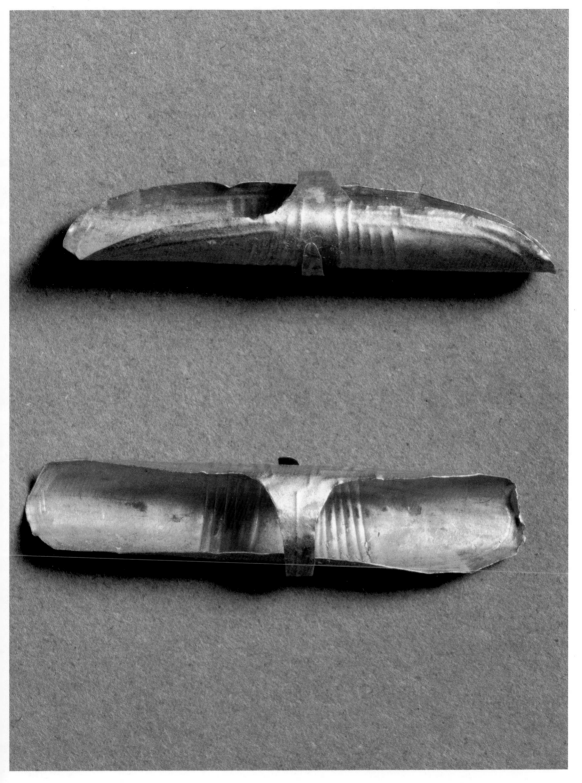

1. Beaker earrings/hair tresses from Barrow 4A, Barrow Hills. (Ashmolean Museum)

2. Gors Fawr stone circle, Pembrokeshire. (Author)

3. Lough Leane, Killarney. (Christophe Meneboeuf)

4. Copper axe-heads and dagger from Ballamoar, Isle of Man. (Manx National Heritage)

5. Grave goods from the Barnack barrow. (British Museum Images)

6. Cup-marked rock, Millstone Burn, Northumberland. (Stan Beckensall)

7. Rock art panel at Dod Law, Northumberland. (Stan Beckensall)

8. Rock art panel at Achnabreck, Kilmartin Glen. (Stan Beckensall)

9. Shrewton 5k Beaker burial, Wiltshire. (Salisbury & South Wiltshire Museum)

10. Cup and ring marks at Ketley Crag rock shelter, Northumberland. (Stan Beckensall)

11. The
Four Stones,
Powys.
(Author)

12. 'Harold's Stones', Trellech. (Martin Powell)

13. Temple Wood stone circle, Kilmartin Glen. (Stan Beckensall)

14. The Folkton drums. (British Museum Images)

15. Decorated chalk plaques found near Stonehenge. (Salisbury & South Wiltshire Museum)

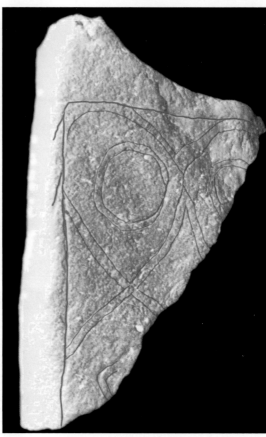

16. The Rothley plaque. (University of Leicester Archaeological Services)

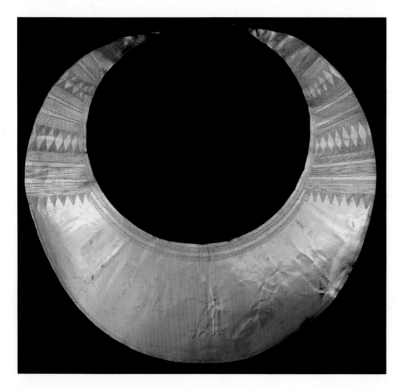

17. 'Provincial' lunula found near Llanllyfni, Llŷn Peninsula. (British Museum Images)

18. Bluestone outcrops on summit of Carn Menyn. (Tim Darvill)

19. Bedd Arthur. (Peter Hodges)

20. Carn Meini ridge seen from bluestone pillar brought down from Carn Menyn by RAF Chinook helicopter. (Author)

21. Chalk block from Durrington Walls with possible copper axe marks. (Mike Parker Pearson)

22. Skara Brae. (Anthony Slegg)

23. Location of arrowhead in Grave 203, Barrow Hills. (Oxford Archaeology Ltd)

24. Beaker bracers from Britain. (From Woodward *et al*. 2006. Photo – John Hunter)

Irish discs are concentrated around the prehistoric copper mines (e.g. Ross Island) in the south-west of the country, and she has made the interesting suggestion that they may have been worn by people involved in the import/export of metals. In light of this idea, it will be recalled that a gold Beaker disc was found in the grave at Banc Tynddol in the Yystwyth Valley (Timberlake 2004, 2009). As mentioned previously, the disc shows some similarities with examples found in northern England, Scotland and Brittany.

Finally there is the unique gold ornament that was discovered near Braithwaite in South Yorkshire (Needham 2001: 14) as a result of metal detecting. It consists of a strip of very flimsy sheet-gold that is slightly crescent-shaped, and which measures some 26cm in length. It is decorated with a series of closely spaced punched dots that run along the edges of the crescent and also around the edges of the small, perforated circular terminals (one of which is snapped off) that would have provided the means by which the ornament was attached to an item of clothing. The form and decoration of this artefact suggest that it was produced by Beaker goldsmiths at some point between *c.* 2500–200 BC.

5

Monuments and Settlements

Like their Neolithic predecessors, and their Bronze Age successors, Britain's Copper Age communities have left behind countless monuments that provide us with tantalising traces of their religious beliefs and practices. Alongside these monuments, a number of domestic sites have also been discovered, although in terms of numbers and aesthetic impact these settlements often struggle to compete with the former. Nevertheless, they provide us with equally valuable insights into Copper Age life and remind us that it did not always revolve around religion – although one suspects that as in other prehistoric periods, the line between domestic and religious life was somewhat blurred and that the two often intermingled. In this chapter, we will look briefly at both, beginning with the 'mother' of all British prehistoric monuments. As will be seen, opinion is unsurprisingly divided in regard to the primary purpose of this remarkable place.

Stonehenge: a Place for the Dead, or a Place for the Living?

In 1998 in the respected archaeological journal *Antiquity* Mike Parker Pearson (one of Britain's leading prehistorians) and his Madagascan colleague, Ramilisonina, put forward an important theory regarding the true significance of Stonehenge. Drawing on anthropological evidence from Madagascar, where standing stones and megalithic tombs are associated with the ancestors, they suggested that a case could be made for seeing Stonehenge in a similar light. As Parker Pearson and Ramilisonina (*ibid*.: 308) said, 'Stonehenge can be interpreted as belonging to the ancestors, a stone version for the dead of the timber circles used for ceremonials by the living. By extension, Avebury and many other stone monuments of this period can be understood as built for the ancestors in parallel to the wooden monuments constructed for the living'. Parker Pearson and Ramilisonina (*ibid*.: 324) concluded their paper with the statement, '[c]ontrary to recent speculations by archaeologists, New Agers and other groups, the great stone monuments, once built, were largely the domain of the spirit world into which the living rarely entered'.

The idea that Stonehenge was primarily a domain of the ancestral dead is an appealing one, but not everyone was prepared to follow this line of reasoning.

For example, John Barrett and Kathryn Fewster (1998: 849) have argued that its basic premise – that stone is associated with the realm of the ancestors and wood with that of the living – is weakened by evidence such as that seen among the Indian tribes on the north-west coast of America. These tribes 'used wooden totem poles to depict their ancestral genealogies and [also] placed these totem poles adjacent to the wooden houses of the living' (*ibid.*). It can also be noted that similar practices have been recorded among other stateless peoples and for example, the Mapuche of south-central Chile erected wooden statues of the ancestors that functioned as territorial markers (Dillehay 1990: 226). Although agreeing with the idea that there is some connection between ancestors and the stones of Stonehenge, Alasdair Whittle (1998: 853) believes 'that the power of the monument rested both on the way it actively involved people and on the diversity of beliefs and traditions which it presented and tried to eternalize'. It is also quite probable that, at least on occasion, some monuments were built that featured both stone and timber circles. A well-known example of one such possible monument is the Sanctuary (57), which is linked to the Avebury ritual and ceremonial complex by the West Kennet Avenue (the Avenue runs south-east from Avebury to the Sanctuary). Traditionally, the Sanctuary has been interpreted as a two-phase monument consisting of a single setting of multiple timber circles, or as a succession of roofed timber structures, which were replaced by two stone

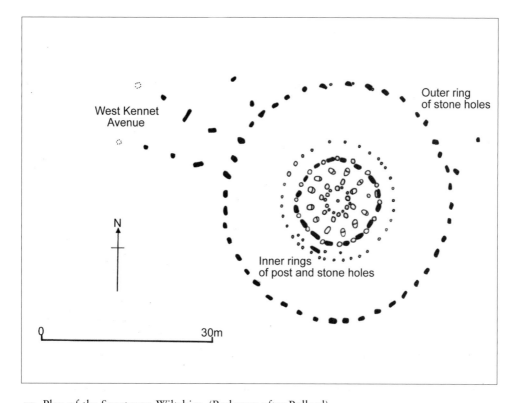

57. Plan of the Sanctuary, Wiltshire. (Redrawn after Pollard)

circles (Pollard 1992: 214). However, it is possible that the Sanctuary was actually constructed as a composite monument featuring both timber and stone circles (dating to *c.* 2500 BC), or perhaps as a two-phase: one of timber then stone (*ibid.*: 224). However, the close conformity of both stone-holes and postholes in ring C suggests that the former is more likely (*ibid.*: 217).

Whatever the truth is in regard to the Sanctuary, the Parker Pearson/ Ramilisonina theory on the significance of Stonehenge undoubtedly generated considerable debate amongst scholars (and continues to do so), and an important result of this debate was that it 'highlighted the gaps in archaeological evidence and the need for a sustained field project to investigate the theory' (Parker Pearson *et al.* 2006: 229). Furthermore, '[i]t had thrown up questions about Stonehenge's relationship with [the nearby] timber circles at Durrington Walls and Woodhenge, [and also] about the significance of the River Avon which potentially linked them as a single complex' (*ibid.*). The Stonehenge Riverside Project thus set out to investigate and resolve these issues and the results it has produced over the last five or so years are undeniably fascinating and have provided us with valuable glimpses of life in prehistoric Britain. There is not space here to provide a detailed account of the discoveries made by the Stonehenge Riverside Project (for a good summary see Parker Pearson *et al.* 2006), but evidence was found to support Parker Pearson's and Ramilisonina's original suggestion that Stonehenge (the circle of the ancestors) and Woodhenge (the circle of the living) may have been distinct but complementary places, linked to each other by the River Avon and the avenue that led down to the river not only from Stonehenge, but also from Durrington Walls as well. As Richard Bradley (2007: 126) has also pointed out, archaeological evidence from elsewhere in Britain lends support to the theory that that timber circles were places for the living, whilst the stone ones were for the dead, as the former are often associated with much richer collections of material culture, pointing to activities such as feasting.

Nonetheless, there is Tim Darvill's (2007: 146) appealing and alternative theory that Stonehenge may have been a renowned healing centre and oracle, rather than a place that was haunted by the ancestors and little visited by the living. As Darvill (*ibid.*: 156) has said in support of his idea, '[a] surprising number of the burials [in the Stonehenge area] of third-millennium BC date, including the Amesbury Archer, were suffering from long-term health problems which they may have hoped would be cured by presenting themselves to the gods at Stonehenge just as pilgrims travelling to Santiago de Compostela hoped for relief during the Middle Ages'. The most interesting aspect of Darvill's theory, however, is his suggestion that it was the smaller Welsh bluestones within Stonehenge that were believed to have healing powers, and which led its builders to create a prehistoric Lourdes in the gently rolling grasslands of Wiltshire (Catling 2007: 12).

However, not all scholars (e.g. Burl 2007: 181–202) agree that the bluestones were somehow transported around 230km from the Preseli Hills in north Pembrokeshire to Salisbury Plain by ingenious prehistoric people who possessed great powers of perseverance. Instead, they argue that it was glaciers that brought

58. Carn Menyn seen from prehistoric trackway. (Author)

the bluestones to Wiltshire many thousands of years before Stonehenge was built. Nevertheless, the majority of archaeologists favour the former idea and while it could be argued that they are ignoring the more mundane reality in a favour of a more romantic, but ultimately untruthful story, the geological evidence seems to suggest otherwise. As Stuart Piggott (1941: 306–307) tells us, '[a]fter various guesses as to [the] origin [of the bluestones], some fairly near the truth, this was definitely established by Dr H. H. Thomas in 1923. From petrological examination by microscopic sections he found that the only place where the stones were matched as a group was the Carn Meini region of the Presely Range in Pembrokeshire, where the various rhyolites and the unique spotted dolerite occur'. In addition to this earlier analysis, modern and sophisticated petrological techniques have backed up Thomas's findings and revealed that most of the dolerites come from the main outcrop, Carn Menyn, (58 & plate 18) and the nearby Carn Goedog, whilst the majority of the rhyolites and tuffs derive from the volcanic outcrops that lie on the periphery of the dolerite carns. Four stones of the central Bluestone Oval/Horsehoe that were sampled by Richard Thorpe and his team from the Open University 'proved to originate in a compact area no more than 3km across centred on Carn Menyn' (Darvill 2007: 137). Contrastingly, the outer 'Bluestone Circle surrounding the central settings is a mish-mash of stones of many different types; the 11 samples studied by the Open University

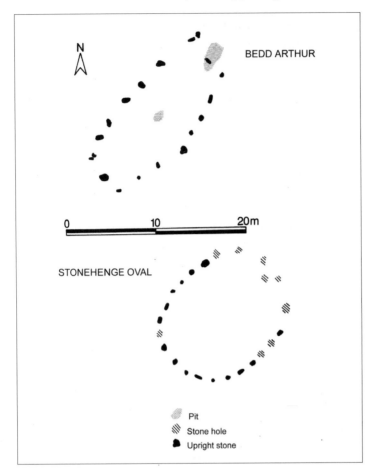

59. Plans of Bedd Arthur & the Stonehenge Oval. (Redrawn after Darvill & Wainwright)

team represented at least eight different sources including dolerites, rhyolites, and tuffs from outcrops scattered over a fairly wide area along and around the main Preseli ridge' (*ibid.*). Recent research has also suggested that some of the 'rhyolitic' bluestones may have come from outcrops at Port Saeson which lies a couple of miles to the north of Carn Menyn (Bevins *et al.* 2011).

In addition to this 'mirroring' of the geology of Carn Meini in the various bluestone arrangements at Stonehenge, there is also the somewhat unusual monument known as Bedd Arthur ('Arthur's Grave'), which lies about half a mile due west of Carn Menyn (plate 19). As has been noted (Darvill & Wainwright 2003: 32), similar monuments to Bedd Arthur exist in the Irish Sea region and beyond, with the nearest one found on Skomer Island off the Pembrokeshire coast. Intriguingly, however, Bedd Arthur appears to more closely resemble the inner Bluestone Oval/ Horseshoe at Stonehenge. In fact, it has been credibly suggested (Darvill 2007: 139) that the two monuments are of such a similar shape, size and orientation 'that [they] must be closely connected, if not the work of the same people' (59). Furthermore, investigations in 2004 by the SPACES (Strumble-Preseli Ancient Communities and Environment Study) discovered an ancient quarry on the summit of Carn Menyn and broken bluestone monoliths of very similar proportions to those erected at Stonehenge were found lying scattered about this area (*ibid.*).

Of course, there will still be those who argue in favour of the glacial action theory for the presence of the bluestones at Stonehenge, but it appears to be the case that they argue in vain. As Mike Pitts (2001: 204) has pointed out, the debate over the origin of the bluestones should have been settled many years ago, as a study made by Christopher Green in the early 1970s revealed a complete lack of glacial material in river gravels in Wiltshire and Hampshire.

It can be seen, then, that there is very strong evidence (if not proof) to support the widely held belief that bluestones were quarried from the Preseli Hills and then transported to Stonehenge. However, the same cannot perhaps be said for the theory that this mammoth task was undertaken because it was believed that the bluestones could heal the sick. Mike Pitts (2009: 191) tells us, '[a]mongst British prehistorians, and beyond those working with Darvill and Wainwright, I have found it hard to identify anyone prepared to offer strong support to the healing stones idea'.

Intriguingly, though, it could be possible that there is ancient literary evidence to support Darvill's bluestone theory. The Welsh monk, Geoffrey of Monmouth, records in his twelfth-century *Historia Regum Britanniae* ('History of Britain') that giant stones with healing powers were taken from Ireland by the Dark Age ruler, Aurelius Ambrosius (who was aided by Merlin), and subsequently erected on Salisbury Plain (Piggot 1941: 306). Undoubtedly, such accounts should be treated with caution and Geoffrey's work certainly contains much 'jumbled myth, legend and fantasy' (*ibid.* 305). It has, though, been reasonably argued (Darvill 2007: 137) that underneath all this fantastical fiction 'are the critical ideas that some at least of Stonehenge was brought from a land far to the west and set up on Salisbury Plain … [and] that the stones themselves were regarded as having special powers'. It is also perhaps of some interest that local folklore attributes the many springs around Carn Meini with healing properties, and the SPACES team has found evidence that some of these springs were artificially modified to create walled pools, which seem to be associated with nearby prehistoric rock art and cairns (Catling 2007: 18).

Exactly when the bluestones arrived at Stonehenge can obviously never be completely pinned down but the traditional view is that it was around 2500 BC, although as has been pointed out (Darvill 2007: 119), it is not known '[w]hether [they] arrived gradually over a long period of time, or were the result of a concerted effort to get the raw materials for this project'. A recent reinterpretation of the Stonehenge structural sequence (Mike Parker Pearson *et al.* 2008: 26, Table 1) has challenged the idea that the bluestones arrived at Stonehenge in the middle of the third millennium BC. Instead, it has been argued (*ibid.*: 32) that the Aubrey Holes, which have traditionally been thought to have held the posts of a timber circle set up inside the earlier henge, are – to judge by their overall appearance – more likely to have held at least fifty-six Welsh bluestones. A recent discovery made by the Stonehenge Riverside Project should also be briefly mentioned here, as it may have implications for the architectural sequence of events at Stonehenge and could also provide remarkable evidence that another bluestone circle once existed near West Amesbury (some 3 miles north-east of Stonehenge), at the junction of the River Avon and the Stonehenge Avenue (Catling 2009). Returning to further investigate a henge that they had uncovered in 2008, the project excavated a quarter of this monument in the summer of 2009 and inside its external bank and inner ditch (which was at least *c.* 25m in diameter) nine large circular pits were also discovered. These seemed to be too wide and shallow to support timber posts, and thus the plausible conclusion reached was that they represented the remains of a dismantled stone circle that had originally consisted of around twenty-five stones. Two 'Petit Tranchet Derivative' arrowheads were found in packing deposits, giving a rough date of *c.* 3400–2500 BC for the construction of the monument. Interestingly, it could be possible that the stones from 'Bluestonehenge' (as this new monument has been dubbed) were later removed from their location on the banks of the River Avon and transported to Stonehenge. Here, along with the fifty-six bluestones that may originally have stood in the Late Neolithic Aubrey Holes, they could have been incorporated into the various bluestone settings that were arranged within Stonehenge *c.* 2550–2000 BC. It is interesting to note in light of this theory that some eighty bluestones feature in these settings. Also of some interest is the fact that radiocarbon dates obtained on two antler picks found at the monument indicate that Bluestonehenge was moved between 2480 and 2280 BC (Mike Parker Pearson pers. comm.).

Ancestors Enshrined in Stone?

Tim Darvill (2007: 140) has made the credible suggestion that the Preseli Hills may have been perceived as the home of the gods or the ancestors by the people who moved the bluestones to Stonehenge (one also suspects that earlier and later prehistoric communities viewed these hills as sacred). Christopher Catling (2007: 16) has also put forward the plausible idea that the striking rock outcrops or carns that form the Carn Meini ridge 'might in the past, have been seen as the work of deities or heroic ancestors – gigantic versions of the chambered tombs and passage graves built by the Neolithic people for their own dead'. As Catling (*ibid.*) further says of the Carn Meini ridge '[t]he atmosphere of a liminal place between earth and sky is enhanced by the evocative, primordial shapes of the rocky outcrops that form the "walls and towers" of this city in the clouds' (plate 20). It is description that nicely captures the unique quality of this striking and beautiful corner of north Pembrokeshire, which must surely have been viewed very differently by people who had no knowledge of how natural geological processes could produce what is – even to the modern visitor – a haunting and otherworldly place. Perhaps then, it was their connection with the powerful supernatural forces that were believed to inhabit Carn Meini that made the bluestones so special, and gave them their powers – healing or otherwise. It could even be possible that they were actually believed to be the gods or ancestors enshrined in stone, who were brought to Stonehenge to help and watch over the living.

Such an idea is brought to mind by the thought-provoking paper of Mark Gillings and Joshua Pollard (1992), which investigates the 'biographies' of the massive sarsen stones that stand inside the awesome henge monument at Avebury, which probably dates from the mid- to late third millennium BC (Gillings & Pollard 2004: 44–49). They suggest (*ibid*.: 182–184) that prior to their erection, these stones may have been venerated as special places in the landscape by the Late Neolithic communities who regularly came across them in the sarsen fields (which would have been much more extensive in this period) of north Wiltshire, and that in time they came to be seen as the embodiment of ancestral spirits. Thus Gillings and Pollard (*ibid*.: 184) propose that with the erection of these stones inside the Avebury henge, rather than being built *for* the ancestors, it was built *of* them, with certain stones identified with specific ancestral entities (*ibid*.: 184).

As already noted above, Parker Pearson and Ramilisonina have drawn an analogy with the ancestor or *vatolahy* stones of Madagascar in their new interpretation of Stonehenge, Avebury, and other contemporary stone monuments, but there are many other examples of this stone-ancestor association found in the ethnographic record. For example, in Wamira, Papua New Guinea, many stones of all shapes and sizes (some arranged in circles, or as a individual standing stones) have mythical significance 'and are said to be the paraphernalia of ancestral heroes or heroines – or the ancestors or ancestresses themselves – that have turned to stone' (Khan 1990: 51). In north-western Cameroon, some stone circles, which were probably erected around AD 1600, have continued in use into modern times as shrines connected with ancestral worship (Asombang 2003). In a slightly different vein, stone tools and weapons used by the Aborigines of western Arnhem Land, Australia, were felt to be more effective and powerful because they were quarried from rocks inhabited or connected with ancestral beings from the Dreamtime (Taçon 1991).

However, leaving aside this brief foray into the ethnographic record, James Whitley (2002) has argued – somewhat vehemently – that archaeologists now turn too readily to the ancestors in their interpretation of British prehistoric monuments. He says (*ibid*: 119), '[a] spectre is haunting British archaeology – the omnipresent ancestor. [They are] the explanation of choice for a whole range of archaeological phenomena, from the siting of monuments within the landscape to the use of stone as opposed to wood in the construction of stone circles and henges ... the universal ancestor has gone from being a suggestion to becoming an orthodoxy without ever having had to suffer the indignity of being treated as a mere hypothesis. Ancestors are everywhere, and everything is ancestral.' Mike Pitts (2003: 1770, however, does not agree: '[n]one of this is "orthodoxy". It is a debate ... ancestors are a considerably more productive thinking tool than the more usual astronomers, priests and mathematicians, or half-naked savages. I see no reason why they should not also constitute a creative arena for archaeology students.'

Beaker 'Builders' at Stonhenge and Avebury?

Discovering the true identity of the people who built Britain's greatest prehistoric monuments lies beyond our reach, but at Stonehenge at least, Humphrey Case (1997: 166) has argued that 'the chronological, stratigraphical and artefactual evidence combine to show that the builders of [its] major stone structures were users of Beaker pottery'. In support of his theory, Case (*ibid*.: 165) notes that Beaker pottery dominates the ceramic sequence at Stonehenge and, furthermore, that Beaker pottery is 'stratigraphically associated with *all* the major phases of stone or intended stone construction'. In addition to this evidence, he argues (*ibid*.) that there is the famous burial of the Beaker archer in the ditch to consider, and the tubular sheet copper or bronze bead found in Aubrey Hole 18, which is similar to the gold example that we saw earlier in the rich Beaker grave at Chilbolton. However, as we will see below, remarkable evidence has recently come to light that perhaps links the building of Stonehenge with people of the Grooved Ware culture, although, of course, this does not necessarily prove that they were the real power behind its construction.

Turning to the Avebury ritual and ceremonial complex, there is also perhaps again evidence indicating that Beaker communities lay behind the erection of some of the megalithic settings here. For example, in the early 1930s, Ben and Maud Cunnington discovered a Beaker burial close to the substantial hole (4m by 2m) that had held the huge sarsen stone known as 'Adam' (the remaining stone of the megalithic setting known as the 'Longstones Cove' that was linked to the western entrance of Avebury by the Beckhampton Avenue), which had crashed into the ground not long before they excavated at Avebury (Pitts 2001: 208–209). At the West Kennet Avenue, a grave containing a cord-decorated Beaker was found at the foot of stone 29a and at the sanctuary itself, a juvenile accompanied by a Beaker was buried immediately in front of stone-hole C12. Of course, these burials may have been made many years after the Avebury complex was built because, as it has been noted (Pitts & Whittle 1992: 210), Beaker pottery is often found at older monuments that predate this distinctive ceramic tradition. Also, if the Sanctuary was a composite monument that featured both stone and timber circles (and as noted above the structural evidence does point in this direction) then the ceramic evidence suggests that it may well have been people of the Grooved Ware culture who lay behind its construction *c*. 2500 BC (Pollard 1992: 213). If this was indeed the case, then they may well have been responsible for the construction of Avebury, or at least the hugely impressive ditch and bank and the henge encircling the stones.

Silbury Hill

Of course, Stonehenge and Avebury are not the only prehistoric monuments that stand on Salisbury Plain as awe-inspiring testaments to their builders; there is also the hugely impressive Silbury Hill, which is the largest artificial mound in prehistoric Europe. It reaches 37m in height, measures 160m across at its base, and it has been estimated that more than 300,000 cubic metres of material were used in its construction (Scarre 1998: 95).

However, whilst archaeology has allowed us glimpses of why Stonehenge and Avebury were constructed, the same cannot be said for Silbury Hill, and this massive mound, which has exercised the imaginations of scholars for hundreds of years, undoubtedly provides us with one of Europe's greatest prehistoric enigmas. As far back as the seventeenth century, John Aubrey recorded in his *Monumenta Britannica* that 'no history gives any account of this hill. The tradition only is that King Sel or Zel, as the country folk pronounce, was buried here on horseback, and that the hill was raised while a posset of milk was seething' (*ibid.*).

It seems unlikely that the true purpose of this huge monument will ever be discovered, as the various investigations that have taken place at Silbury Hill over the last 270 years or so have brought us no nearer to discovering why it was built. Nonetheless, there have been some suggestions as to its function and there can be little doubt that Alisdair Whittle's ranks as one of the most unusual, but nevertheless thought-provoking, ones. He has wondered (2007: 150) whether, rather than being influenced by the design of large, indigenous round mounds and cairns (e.g. Duggleby Howe in Yorkshire and Quanterness or Maes Howe in Orkney), the builders of Silbury Hill looked to much more distant horizons for their inspiration. As Whittle (*ibid*: 150–151) says:

Silbury is not pyramidical in shape, nor did it necessarily share the stepped constructional technique of Djoser's [famous step pyramid], but the whole scale of the enterprise could have owed much to the pre-existence of the early pyramids ... A connection of this kind might have required an individual or individuals to have travelled to Egypt, or communication via third parties. To the same third millennium BC world, but yet further away, belonged the newly created ziggurats of the Early Dynastic period in Mesopotamia. Fashionable consensus presently requires prehistoric people to have been largely rooted in local domesticity, but there is nothing to have prevented individuals moving about ... Had someone from southern Britain seen one of these wonders? Or had word gone down wind of their existence, filtered and embroidered in numerous retellings? And was the construction or elaboration of the mound an annexation of the distant and exotic for political advantage, or an act of devotion to the power of gods or spirits?

Some may feel that Whittle's intriguing ruminations are too far-fetched to be worthy of serious consideration, but as he says (*ibid.*: 150), '[t]he unusual may require unusual explanation'.

Whether or not the builders of Silbury Hill were influenced by the design and ideological purpose of contemporary monuments built by far-distant civilisations is debatable, but one thing that cannot be disputed about Silbury is its flat summit, which measures some 30m in diameter. Therefore, the idea that it was used as a viewing platform and that the prehistoric people who gathered here did so in order to watch the midsummer sun rising over Salisbury Plain is certainly plausible (Scarre 1998: 97). However, Jim Leary (2011: 40) has recently said, 'Silbury's flat top may be a bit of a red herring, and not part of its ancient shape: it seems to have been altered in later periods'. It has also been suggested (Bayliss *et al.* 2007: 50), that Stonehenge and Silbury Hill, may have both been in their different ways 'symbols of cosmic origin or rebirth [and one] may have played off the other, as novel, grandiose conceptions of how the world came into being, promoted and developed in the changing circumstances of the times'. Whatever the truth is in respect of the significance of these two mighty monuments, they will undoubtedly continue to fascinate and frustrate those who seek to understand them, long after we have gone the way of the people who lie behind their construction.

Unsurprisingly, given its resemblance to a giant burial mound, the antiquarian and archaeological investigations at Silbury Hill have mainly focused on finding rich and spectacular burials somewhere inside its huge bulk. Unfortunately, Silbury Hill has not been particularly forthcoming in this regard; in 1776, Colonel Drax and the Duke of Northumberland sunk a shaft from the top of the hill and found a small sliver of oak (perhaps from a coffin) and a 'man' at its base (Chadburn *et al.* 2005: 14). Nevertheless, as Mike Pitts (2001: 192) points out in his engrossing *Hengeworld*, we may still yet discover such burials at Silbury Hill and indeed, he may well be right in his belief that it is 'ready for excavation on a large scale, not least in the ditch, which should prove a treasure house of historical and environmental information' (*ibid.*).

It has been pointed out (Bayliss *et al.* 2007: 43) that we might be tempted to see Silbury Hill (and other major monuments such as Stonehenge) as expressions of a Chiefdom society, as envisaged by Colin Renfrew in his classic book, *Before Civilization*. However, rather than being constructed under the leadership of a dominant figure (or figures) who sat at the head of a centralised authority, it may have been constructed in a more *ad hoc* fashion over a longer period of time, with a succession of charismatic individuals leading a project that was supported by the wider community (*ibid.*: 44). Some weight may be lent to this idea by the new dating programme carried out on earlier and more recent samples of archaeological material taken from Silbury Hill (the latter were obtained when part of the top of the mound collapsed in 2000). This suggests that the huge construction project of Silbury Hill was begun around 2400 BC and was not finally finished until the Early Bronze Age *c.* 2000 BC (*ibid.*: 39–42).

Durrington Walls

Some of the most important discoveries in British Archaeology in recent years have been made by the Stonehenge Riverside Project (*Current Archaeology* 2007; Parker Pearson 2007, 2008; Thomas 2007). In addition to discovering a unique and very substantial avenue (170m long by 30m wide) of trampled flint which ran up from the River Avon through the eastern entrance of the henge to link up with the interior Southern Circle (a two-phase timber monument discovered by Geoffrey Wainwright during his excavations at Durrington Walls in the late 1960s), the remains of several houses came to light. Six of these lay just outside the eastern entrance, with two located on opposite sides of the avenue's banks (these may have served as gatehouses of some sort) and the other four located on a terraced slope just to the north-east. The houses varied in size, with the smallest example measuring just *c.* 3m by 3m and the largest *c.* 6m by 5m. This variation in size perhaps suggests that some houses contained individuals, while others may have been the dwelling places of families, although it appears likely that the smallest house functioned as an ancillary hut. It seems that the houses were mainly constructed using wooden posts or stakes and that they had daub walls covered in chalk plaster.

Archaeological evidence recovered from the interiors of the houses has provided us with rare insights into the domestic lives of the people who lived within these modest structures. For example, in the largest house (House 851), which was also the best preserved, there was a rectangular clay floor and a slightly sunken oval hearth, which lay just off-centre of this floor. The hearth had seen considerable use, as revealed by its well-smoothed contours, and just to the south of the hearth was a shallow double depression, which probably indicated the spot where someone had repeatedly kneeled to cook food or to clean out the ashes from the hearth. These small archaeological details may seem dull to those who want their archaeology to be of the spectacular kind, but it is details such as these that perhaps provide us with our strongest connection to the people of the distant past. The series of slots also discovered in the floor of House 851 probably represented the footings of a box bed and a small cupboard or dresser. House 851 also provided possible evidence of a possible ritual deposition, as a small pit containing animal bones and an arrowhead were discovered in between the doorway stakeholes.

In house 547, another well-used hearth was found, along with further evidence for the presence of interior furniture in the form of a box bed or dresser. House 547 also featured a clay floor that showed signs of heavy burning over much of its surface, and concentrations of burnt flint tools, arrowheads, Grooved Ware sherds and bone fragments lay on it. A section of articulated cattle vertebrae lay close to the edge of the hearth and an articulated pig's trotter was found lying on the clay floor at the northern end of the house. It may be interesting to note that these houses invite close comparisons to those found in the famous Orcadian settlement of Skara Brae, which was occupied from the Late Neolithic to the end of the Copper Age *c.* 3000–2200 BC.

Two buildings excavated within the western interior of the henge may also have been houses, as they were similar in size and shape to those found near the eastern entrance and both contained hearths. These hearths showed up on a magnetometer survey undertaken in the western interior as small anomalies, which marked the location of their baked floors. It is possible, however, that these buildings had a non-domestic function, as their interiors were lacking household waste and thus they may have been shrines or cult-houses of some sort. Whatever the case, the fact that many hundreds of other similar anomalies were also highlighted by this survey suggests that the Durrington Walls settlement was of a very substantial size and that many hundreds of people lived here.

One of the most interesting possibilities thrown up by discovery of the Durrington Walls settlement is that it housed the workers who were involved in the construction of Stonehenge. The settlement appears to have been built *c.* 2600–2500 BC and it will be recalled from Chapter 1 that a strong case has recently been put forward for the construction of Stonehenge in the twenty-sixth, rather than the twenty-fifth century BC. The idea that the builders of Stonehenge perhaps inhabited the Durrington Walls settlement gains further weight when it is considered that the evidence indicates that, unusually for the time, the settlement was home to a very large community of people who could have numbered in their thousands. However, there are other possibilities that spring to mind when considering the identity of the Durrington Walls community. Perhaps one of the most plausible is that they were prehistoric pilgrims who came to Stonehenge to participate in the important religious rituals and ceremonies that probably took place here during the midwinter and midsummer solstices. Whoever they were, it seems the inhabitants of Durrington Walls lived well, as many thousands of animal bones (mainly pig and cattle – the former were mostly culled in the midwinter, and both species seem to have been brought to the village from outside) were found scattered over the ground surface of this Grooved Ware settlement. Interestingly, many of the pig bones had broken-off arrow tips embedded in them, which many indicate that archers were involved in sporting competitions that displayed their prowess with the bow. With this idea in mind, it may be interesting to note here that the ceremonies carried out in the war temples of the ancient Hawaiians culminated in the killing and consumption of hundreds of pigs (Kolb & Dixon 2002: 518). The people of the village also seem to have supplemented their diets with hazelnuts and crab apples, although no cereal evidence pointing to the consumption of bread or alcohol was recovered from any of the houses.

Intriguing evidence hinting that copper axes may well have been in use in the twenty-sixth century BC was also found at Durrington Walls. Shortly after the settlement at Durrington Walls was abandoned, the massive ditch of this 'super-henge' was dug out, and discovered within it was a chalk block displaying cut-marks that look very much like they have been made by a copper axe (plate 21). Unfortunately, no other evidence for the use of metal tools has been found at Durrington Walls, aside from green staining seen on animal bones, which has revealed low levels of copper. It is more probable, though, that this was naturally absorbed from the environment.

Interestingly, recent excavations at Marden henge (also in Wiltshire, and Britain's largest 'super-henge') have uncovered similar evidence to that seen at Durrington Walls. Not only has a broad trackway running down from the henge to the River Avon come to light, but a probable Grooved Ware house has also been discovered on top of the henge bank (*Current Archaeology* 2010). This rectangular structure (around 4m by 3m) has four postholes at its corners marking former roof supports, cavities within its floor indicating the positions of cupboards or shrines, and a small outer chalk platform that may possibly mark the remnants of a verandah. Although only the top layers of the middens associated with the structure were excavated, an abundance of Grooved Ware sherds, bone pins and awls, pig bones, flint tools and two very fine flint arrowheads were found.

Beaker Settlements

Like their Grooved Ware counterparts, Beaker domestic sites are somewhat rare in Britain, but nevertheless, evidence recovered from the chalk downloads of southern England suggests that this area of Britain at least saw a fair level of occupation by Beaker communities, who built their settlements in valley bottoms (Allen 2005). The best known of these southern English sites is Belle Tout, which is located in a dry valley on the chalk cliff-tops near Beachy Head in East Sussex (the southern part of the site has been almost destroyed because of cliff erosion). Although Belle Tout has attracted interest from other archaeologists, it is Richard Bradley who has carried out the most thorough archaeological investigation of the site (1970). Although the picture of Beaker occupation at Belle Tout is not completely clear, Bradley's excavations revealed evidence for successive periods of occupation at the site. These occupation areas were surrounded by two overlapping earthwork enclosures consisting of low outer banks and wide internal ditches. These enclosures may have been used to contain livestock, although somewhat curiously, the remains of no domesticated animals were found at the site. Although rather meagre in character, the remains of several houses were found, and the earliest of these dwellings were associated with AOC Beakers. Large quantities of sherds from 'East Anglian style' Beakers were discovered in association with the later houses and impressions from emmer wheat and barley were found in some of the earlier and later sherds, pointing to the cultivation of crops nearby. In further respect of the Belle Tout agricultural economy, it is quite possible that some of the pits found on the site were used for storing grain. An extensive flint industry was seen on all parts of the site and included scrapers (found in abundance), knives, barbed and tanged arrowheads, pounding stones, and knives or sickles bearing occasional traces of silica goss – testifying to their use in the harvesting of crops. The large numbers of scrapers found at Belle Tout may also indicate that the large-scale preparation of animal hides took place here.

Across the Irish Sea, Beaker settlements have been discovered at Lough Gur, Ballynagilly, Monknewtown, and Dalkey Island (Waddell 2000: 117), but it is from close to the famous Newgrange passage grave that we perhaps have our best evidence for Beaker settlement in Ireland. John Waddell (*ibid.*: 117–118) has provided a useful summary of the abundant evidence that was found near this hugely impressive Neolithic tomb. Although no definitive house plans were identified, some seventeen hearths (often rectangular in form and edged by carefully laid stones) were discovered, along with many pits, post-holes and short lengths of foundation trenches. Numerous Beaker sherds, flint tools (scrapers were the most common), and animal bones were recovered from the site, and in one of three oval pits, charred grains of wheat and barley were dated to *c.* 2480–2280 BC. A boulder discovered close to one of the hearths (some of which may have been outdoors) showed heavy signs of wear, and it is possible that it was used as a metalworker's anvil. The animal remains predominately consisted of cattle and pig bones, although small numbers of sheep or goat bones and bones from a domestic dog were also identified. It is also interesting to note that horse bones were discovered at the site, although it has to be admitted that it is not certain that these came from a domesticated animal. Nevertheless, it may be possible that Beaker people rode small horses similar to the mustangs of the Native American Comanches, and it could be, perhaps, that horses played a significant part in the rapid and widespread dissemination of Beakers across Europe (Burl 1987: 108). Small quantities of wild animal bones were also found at the site, and included wild cat, brown bear, wild boar and red deer.

It should also be mentioned that not everybody has been prepared to accept that the above evidence is indicative of domestic activity, and, for example, Charles Mount (1994) has argued that it actually represents the traces of ritual activities that took place in the shadow of this awesome prehistoric monument.

Ronaldsway

As mentioned previously, the Ronaldsway culture of the Isle of the Man spanned much of the third millennium BC and the type-site of this culture, the 'Ronaldsway house', appears to date to the earlier stages of the Copper age *c.* 2400 BC (Darvill & Burrow 1997, Table 2; Tim Darvill pers. comm.). This important site, which confirmed the existence of a new British 'Neolithic' culture, was discovered by chance in 1943 during the extension of the Isle of Man airport on the northern shore of Ronaldsway Bay (Bruce *et al.* 1947).

The house (one end of which had been destroyed) was rectangular and measured *c.* 7.5m long by 4m wide (60). Its floor was slightly sunken below the old land surface and featured a central hearth, with postholes marking the timbers that had supported the roof, which was probably thatched. Just to the east of the hearth, the occupants of the house had dug a hole, into which they placed the long bones of an ox before covering it with a large horizontal slab. A small and intact flat-based pot was also discovered alongside the bones and it seems likely that the deliberate burial of these items represents a ritual deposit of some kind.

Other flat-based pots were included amongst the finds from the house and sherds from at least fifty other vessels, some of which had belonged to the large and robust round-bottomed jars, which are a distinctive characteristic of the Ronaldsway culture. Small amounts of Grooved Ware sherds were also possibly present amongst the pottery assemblage from the house (Tim Darvill pers. comm.). Numerous sheep and ox bones were scattered over the floor of

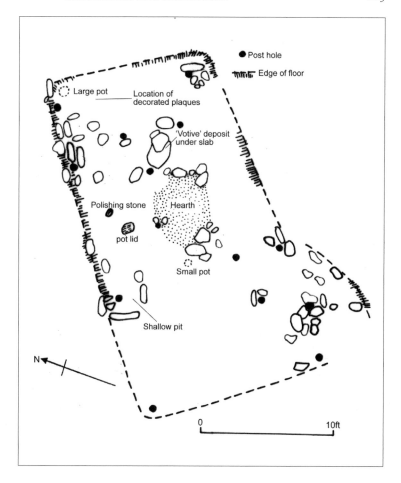

Post hole

Edge of floor

Large pot

Location of decorated plaques

'Votive' deposit under slab

Polishing stone

Hearth

pot lid

Small pot

Shallow pit

N

60. Plan of Ronaldsway House. (Redrawn after Bruce & Megaw)

0   10ft

the house, the bones and teeth of a domestic pig, a few cormorant bones and, rather curiously, the upper part of a human femur. In addition to this ceramic and skeletal evidence, there were many stone tools, including seven polished axe-heads, the butt-ends of which were left unpolished and in some cases, deliberately roughened – presumably to aid in their hafting. Small flint axes or adzes were also found, along with flint knives, arrowheads, scrapers, grinding stones, and hammers and mauls. Also discovered were five curious slate plaques and, as seen earlier, two of these featured decoration.

Although the above evidence may well represent the occupation debris from a Manx Copper Age dwelling, we should perhaps bear in mind the possibility that this 'house' was actually a special structure of some sort that had a non-domestic function. As its excavators themselves have noted (*ibid.*: 146) '[c]onsidering that virtually all the finds came from the floor of a single house, part of which was destroyed before investigation could begin, a rather unusual quantity of material was recovered'. The discovery of the human femur fragment may also be interesting in light of the idea that the Ronaldsway structure had a special purpose.

Settlements of the Far North

Although they are relatively unknown, the last settlements that we will briefly examine have provided us with fascinating evidence of domestic life in the far north of Britain during the Copper Age. At the Scord of Brouster, Shetland, excavations were carried out at a series of three prehistoric houses that were associated with field systems and stone boundary walls (Whittle *et al.* 1987). Analysis of the plant remains found at the site clearly revealed that barley was the main crop at the settlement. The archaeological investigation of the settlement revealed that it was occupied for many hundreds of years, with people living and working here from *c.* 3300–1700 BC. Around 2500 BC, an oval house with walls made from stone and earth was constructed over an earlier occupation area (*c.* 2750 BC), the nature of which is unclear. In the house's interior, there are six prominent recesses or alcoves set into the walls, which would have been used as working, sleeping and probably storage areas. The house was later remodelled and, for the next five hundred years or so, it continued to be occupied by different generations of prehistoric farmers, perhaps all of the same bloodline.

The stone tools and other artefacts found within its walls provide valuable insights into the daily lives of the people who had lived here. Included amongst the finds are several stone points and the fact that many are broken or worn probably testifies to their use as prehistoric ploughshares or ards. Several stone axes and clubs were also recovered and the fine quality of the latter may indicate that they had had a ceremonial function of some sort, although the fact that many were clearly broken and chipped on their ends perhaps suggests that it is more likely they had a utilitarian purpose. Several smaller stone tools and the quartz cores from which they had been struck were also recovered from the house along with Stonehouse Ware sherds, a broken bowl made from steatite, and a couple of sandstone discs with chipped edges. As with similar discs found at other sites, it is possible that the examples found at House 1 were used as pot lids, although they seem rather small in this respect.

Several prehistoric houses can also be found not far from the Scord of Brouster, at Stanydale and Gruting (Calder 1955–56). Evidence found at these thick-walled oval structures suggests that they date from the Late Neolithic to the Early Bronze Age Amongst this evidence were the large quantities of the distinctive Stonehouse Ware pottery found in House 1 at Ness of Gruting. As Audrey Henshall (*ibid.*: 383) says of this pottery, 'it seems that beakers must be the prototype for the group of small flat-based vessels which are characterised by slightly convex necks and concave collar immediately above the gentle expansion for the shoulder' (61). Some of the common motifs seen on the pottery such as zones of lattice and herringbone decoration may also have been derived from Beaker pottery. Beaker influence might also be suggested by the miniature and full-size battle axes that were found in House 1, as these were introduced into Britain with the arrival of the Beaker culture, although they perhaps more closely resemble examples found in burials of the famous Early Bronze Age 'Wessex culture' of southern England. Other finds from the houses include hammerstones, querns, polished stone axes, a quartz leaf-shaped arrowhead, a steatite button or bead, stone discs, lumps of pumice (evidently used as rubbing stones of some sort), knives, stone balls of unknown purpose, and ox, sheep and horse bones. Although probably dating to the Early Bronze Age, one of the most interesting finds from the Gruting and Stanydale houses came from the second phase of the Ness of Gruting house and consisted of a large heap (28 lb/12.7 kg) of carbonised barely, which has been dated to *c.* 2000 BC (Turner 1998: 36).

There is also the archaeological evidence recovered from the largest 'house' at Stanydale to consider, which has been summarised by Val Turner (*ibid.*: 44–46 – for a more detailed account of this fascinating site see Calder 1949–50). An AOC Beaker sherd found within this structure suggests that it was built between *c.* 2500 and 2000 BC and sherds of Iron Age pottery also came from the building – suggesting that it may still have been in use over a thousand years later. Although the Stanydale building is similar in character to many of the prehistoric houses on Shetland, it is twice the size of any of these and measures 12m by 7 m, with massive blocks forming walls that are an impressive 4–5m thick. As with many of the other Shetland houses, the building also has six recesses or alcoves, but these are also much bigger than normal. No central hearth is evident, although ash piles from several small fires were found in front of the alcoves, but in contrast to many of the Shetland houses, the floor was free of domestic waste. The few artefacts discovered in the building include fragments from a 'Shetland knife'; it is believed that these flat and highly polished oval discs were primarily ceremonial in purpose. It seems very likely then, judging from the evidence, that the impressive building at Stanydale had a religious function. In fact, Charles Calder's suggestion that it was a prehistoric temple is probably not that far from the truth, although it seems unlikely that it was ultimately inspired by the Neolithic temples found on Malta, as he further suggested (1949–50: 203).

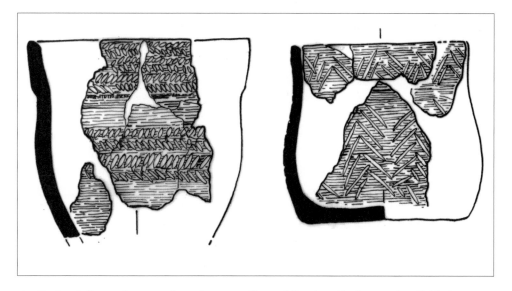

61. Beaker-influenced pottery from House 1, Ness of Gruting. (Redrawn after Calder)

The Scottish 'Pompeii'

As interesting as the above sites are, they are rightly overshadowed by the famous Grooved Ware settlement of Skara Brae on Orkney, which has provided us with such a compelling picture of life in late prehistoric Scotland. The site was occupied for about a thousand years, from the Late Neolithic to the end of the Copper Age, *c.* 3200–2200 BC, although the best-preserved houses are those belonging to the final stages of settlement (plate 22). This remarkable time capsule has provided us with a wealth of archaeological information on the daily lives of this long-lived prehistoric coastal settlement (Childe & Paterson 1929; Childe 1930, 1931; Clarke & Sharples 1985; Ritchie 1995; 30–36; Scarre 1998) and the site is undoubtedly one of Europe's most remarkable archaeological treasures.

The excellent preservation of the later houses of the village reveals that they all follow a uniform plan, with a central stone-kerbed hearth, and stone beds and cupboards or 'dressers' (62). Interestingly, the right-hand beds are always bigger than those on the left, and such an arrangement can be seen in the much later Hebridean black-houses, with the larger bed belonging to the man and the smaller to the woman. It is possible that, as in the black-houses, the occupants of the Skara Brae houses used their dressers as places where they could display objects proclaiming their status, or perhaps they held symbolic objects of the ancestors, or of deities who watched over the people of the village. Of course, the dressers may simply have been used for storing everyday household items, but the fact that they are always located directly opposite the doors of the houses may indicate that they had a more important function. The original appearance of the roofs of the houses is unclear, but it is probable that they comprised of timber frameworks (probably made from driftwood) covered with turf, or thatch. The discovery of whale bones in House 1 during early excavations at the site suggests that these may also have been used as rafters, at least in some houses. A whale's skull was also found in the midden, which lay above one of the passages of the village. The oil and blubber from whales and seals might have been used as fuel for lamps and their skins could perhaps have been used for waterproof clothing. Whether whales were actually hunted by the people of Skara Brae is unlikely (but not impossible) and it is more probable that they scavenged from whale carcasses that must have been washed up from time to time on nearby beaches.

Houses 7 and 8 seem to have been buildings of special status, as suggested by their unique features. Unlike the houses in the main part of the village, which are linked by a main passage, access to House 7 is by a side passage; in further contrast to the other houses, its door would have been barred not from the inside, but from the outside. An earlier stone-built grave featuring two adult females lay underneath the right-hand bed and wall of the house and it is quite possible that they were buried in some sort of foundation ritual. Gordon Childe (1929: 257) has said of these two women from the distant past, '[i]t is surely not far-fetched to regard the individuals thus buried with a minimum of funerary gifts under the walls … as victims of a foundation sacrifice'. We may like to think that this was not the case, but it does remain a disturbing possibility, as this practice has been attested in several ancient cultures around the world. It is also of some interest that a cattle skull was found lying on the right-hand bed, placed there by unknown hands thousands of years ago, probably in a ritual act of some sort. Amongst the suggestions as to what actually went on inside the stone walls of House 7 are that it was used as a place of punishment or initiation or as a place for women who were menstruating or giving birth. We will never know the reality, but the fact that its door was shut from the outside surely reveals that it was a place where people were confined, willingly or not.

House 8 stood alone on the west side of the village and inside there was a central hearth, shelves and cupboards, but no beds, although there were large wall recesses that could have been used as sleeping areas. However, it seems more probable that the main purpose of the building was non-domestic as it differed in design from the other houses in the village and it also lacked everyday household items. It is quite possible that House 8 was a flint-knapper's workshop, as suggested by Childe, as numerous small scrapers and much debris from chert working was found on its floor. There were also heaps of burnt volcanic stone and a possible flue in the north end of the building. This evidence perhaps indicates that the chert was pre-heated in order to improve its flaking qualities. However, although House 8 may have been used as a manufacturing place for stone tools, this does not rule out the possibility that it also functioned as a ceremonial or ritual building.

In further respect of the idea that House 8 had a special function, it is worth noting that like House 7, it contains carved decoration on its interior walls. No other houses in the settlement feature such carvings and most of the decoration at Skara Brae was found on passage walls, and also on some portable artefacts (such as the previously mentioned Skaill knife). Therefore, it seems likely that the carvings seen in Houses 7 and 8 were used as a way of further expressing the special nature of these buildings and, in turn, this suggests that the decoration seen elsewhere at Skara Brae was not simply carved in order to prettify the settlement.

The evidence for subsistence at Skara Brae came mainly from the midden deposits that surrounded and insulated the houses and these deposits revealed that its inhabitants kept cattle, sheep, goats, and small numbers of pigs. It also evident that there were dogs in the village and some of the cattle would have been as large as their extinct predecessors, the aurochs. Red deer also seem to have been occasionally hunted by the Skara Brae villagers, as evidenced by the discovery of small numbers of bones belonging to this species. It is apparent that cereal crops were grown too, with barley providing the main crop of the village, although some wheat was grown as well.

It is not surprising that Skara Brae's inhabitants also made good use of the rich sea-larder that sat on their doorstep and huge numbers of limpet shells and fish bones (mainly from cod and saithe) were recovered from the middens. Unfortunately, no traces of boats survive at Skara Brae, but they must have been

62. Interior of Skara Brae house. (Sigurd Towrie)

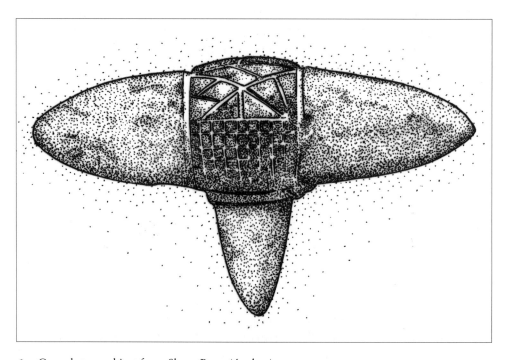

63. Carved stone object from Skara Brae. (Author)

used in order to catch the cod and saithe, which are deep-water fish. Crabs, and oysters were eaten too and the middens contained an abundance of limpet shells, although it is perhaps more probable that these were used as bait to catch cod and saithe, rather than being another item on the villagers marine menu. The people at Skara Brae also ate birds, as shown by the bones of gannet, great auk, shag and guillemot found at the site; fragments of eider duck egg-shell were also identified.

An abundant collection of intriguing objects were found at Skara Brae, including bowls and cups made from whale vertebrae, and stone and bone pots still containing traces of red pigment (which was probably obtained from lumps of haematite found in the village), perhaps indicating that its occupants decorated their bodies with red paint. However, it should be pointed out that excavations at the remarkable religious complex (dated to *c*. 3200–2400 BC) recently discovered at the Ness of Brodgar, Orkney, have revealed that two buildings were painted with red, black and yellow zigzag motifs (*British Archaeology* 2010). Also discovered at Skara Brae were thousands of beads, pendants, and ornamental pins made from animal bones, teeth and tusks, which clearly reveal that the people of Skara Brae liked to wear 'jewellery' (some pieces were quite probably charms or talismans of some sort). Although the material on which they had been strung had unsurprisingly long since disappeared, a few probable examples of whole necklaces and bracelets were also recovered from the houses. The houses also yielded several highly curious and superbly made decorated stone objects, such as the T-shaped implement with each projection ground to a cone, which displays the exceptional skills, creativity, and patience of its prehistoric maker (63). There was even probable evidence of the lighter side of life at Skara Brae, as somewhat remarkably what appear to be bone dice were discovered in one of the houses. Finds of a rarer nature were made in the waterlogged midden that lay on the northern edge of the settlement, such as short lengths of rope made from twisted heather stems, and the remains of puff-balls (the fungus *Bovista nigrescens*). Puff-balls contain a fibrous material that is similar to cotton wool, and in more recent times, they have been used to help clot blood in minor wounds; it is perhaps possible that the people of Skara Brae also used them for this purpose.

Those of us of a more romantic nature may like to envisage the abandonment of Skara Brae around four and a half thousand years ago as being due to some sudden disaster suddenly sweeping down on the settlement, but the reality is probably more mundane, with the gradually encroaching sea and ever-present wind-blown sand and sea-spray the more likely culprits. Not only would it have been hard to grow crops, but the very fields themselves, in which the Skara Brae villagers grew their crops and grazed their animals, were being increasingly threatened by the Atlantic waves, and so they probably finally decided that enough was enough and moved elsewhere. However, if this was indeed the case, then we might still wonder why the people of Skara Brae left so many fine items behind, some of which were probably prized possessions that would have taken many hours to make.

6

WARFARE

The savage has to drive off the wild beasts which attack him, and in turn he hunts and destroys them. But his most dangerous foes are those of his own species, and thus in the lowest known levels of civilisation war has already begun, and is carried on against man with the same club, spear, and bow used against wild beasts.

(Tylor in Davie 1923: 3)

Some people may still view prehistoric Britain in a somewhat golden light, believing that life during this time was essentially peaceful. However, although numerous strands of archaeological evidence have revealed that British prehistoric communities were clearly not 'lowly savages', they have also shown that warfare was an unwelcome but not infrequent visitor among Britain's various prehistoric societies (Heath 2009). Like much of the warfare seen in stateless societies around the world, that of the prehistoric period would have generally been somewhat *ad hoc* and small-scale in nature, consisting mainly of hit-and-run raids (many of which probably took place at night or dawn) skirmishes and ambushes (although larger-scale 'battles' involving many combatants may not have been totally unknown). Nevertheless, this does not mean that it did not impact on communities, and in fact, it seems that 'primitive warfare' was actually more destructive and deadly than its modern, 'civilised' counterpart. As Lawrence Keeley (1997: 88) says in his influential *War Before Civilization*:

[C]itzens of modern states tend to believe that everything they do is more efficient and effective than the corresponding efforts of primitives or ancients ... this expectation about modern civilization finds ready acceptance in relation to distasteful or harmful behaviour. Therefore it comes as something of a shock to discover the proportion of war casualties in primitive societies almost always exceeds that suffered by even the most bellicose of war-torn modern societies.

Not all may agree with this statement, but in support of his argument Keeley provides graphs showing war fatality rates (percentage of population killed per annum) and percentages of male war deaths in prehistoric, primitive, and civilised societies (*ibid.*: 89–90, Figure 6.1, 6.2). It is clear that in both cases, it is the civilised societies who show much lower percentages of war deaths. For further data pertaining to the significant impact that warfare had amongst small-scale, stateless societies see Gat 1999: 574–576. We may perhaps find this surprising, but it should be borne in mind that in stateless societies with low population levels, what we would equate as small loss of life would actually represent the opposite, particularly when set against the cumulative effects of the frequent bouts of warfare that took place in such societies (Keeley 1996: 91). It should also be borne in mind that limited evidence for prehistoric warfare does not necessarily mean that it was low-level in intensity, and therefore was of little consequence to prehistoric communities. Indeed, as George Milner (2005: 145) has remarked:

> [C]onsidering the nature of the archaeological record, the opposite position could also be argued. Even a small proportion of skeletons showing signs of trauma such as projectile wounds [and] fractures attributable to stone axes ...are a sure sign that fighting was pervasive and quite conceivably had a noticeable impact on participating communities.

As will be seen below, evidence such as this can be found in the archaeological record of Copper Age Britain although, of course, other possibilities such as murder, execution and even accidental death should not be ignored when signs of violent death are seen. Also, just because the ethnographic record supports the case for the importance and prevalence of warfare amongst stateless societies in many areas of the world, this cannot be taken as proof that a similar situation existed in Copper Age Britain. However, while it would be wrong to conclude this book by portraying Britain at this time as a brutal and bloody island plagued by constant warfare, archaeological evidence strongly suggests that warfare was certainly not unknown. It can also be argued that it is likely that many more people than we might assume lost their lives as a result of armed conflicts during this period, even though these individuals are archaeologically invisible. Though this cannot be proved for certain, it is hard to disagree with Milner (1999: 110) who has said in regard to these unrecognised victims of prehistoric warfare:

> [T]he bodies of people who died far away from their village would not always be found and returned for burial, particularly if the deaths took place deep in enemy territory. For victims interred in village cemeteries, it is by no means sure that their violent deaths would be detected because lethal wounds often do not leave distinctive marks on bones. Incomplete skeletons and poor bone preservation further reduce the recognition of casualties.

In a similar vein, Meyer *et al.* (2009) have stated:

> The number of lethal injuries in the archaeological record is certainly much higher than can be recognized from osteological analyses alone, especially in the case of arrow injuries. Although massive cranial trauma certainly has a high chance to damage bone and is thus recognized more easily in archaeological human remains,

bad preservation of the bones may mask or destroy these signs, which also leads to an underestimation of violence in prehistory.

'Casualties of War': Possibilities

Stonehenge is one of the world's most famous prehistoric monuments, and many people are aware of this amazing testament to prehistoric life, even if they have little or no interest in the distant past. However, it is likely that many people are unaware that the monument has also yielded grim but fascinating evidence relating to the darker side of life in Copper Age Britain (Atkinson & Evans 1978; Evans 1984; Burl 2007).

In 1978, archaeologists digging near the north-east entrance to Stonehenge accidentally uncovered a crudely dug grave (dating to *c.* 2300 BC) in the ditch that encircles the massive stones. In the grave lay the skeleton of a healthy and well-built young man, aged around twenty-five years, who had clearly not departed the prehistoric world peacefully, as arrowhead tips were found lodged in the back of his sternum and in one of his ribs. One of the ribs in his lower left back also had a deep groove on it, very probably marking the point of entry of the arrowhead that was embedded in the young man's breastbone. As John Evans (1984: 17) tells us, '[t]his was the fatal wound, the arrow entering the back on the left side, hitting the edge of the rib and being deflected upwards, almost certainly passing through the heart before reaching the sternum'. Further damage seen on another rib indicated that another arrow had been fired into the young man's body. In fact, the skeletal evidence strongly suggests that he was killed at close range by more than one assailant, as the arrows do not appear to show a downward penetration that would be expected from a falling arrow. It also appears probable that that he had been attacked from behind, and from his left and right also.

Lying along the inner face of the man's lower arm was a bracer made from a dark grey fine-grained rock, which was somewhat slate-like in character (64). Where the rock came from to make the bracer is unknown, but similar bracers have been found in Britain, with the majority coming from Scotland and County Antrim. Three of the four (or more) barbed and tanged arrowheads that had been fired at this mysterious individual were found in close association with his skeleton (65) and all had broken tips. The remainder of the arrowhead that had been fired into his sternum was not found. In his report on the discovery, Evans (*ibid.*: 19) makes the pertinent comment that '[w]hile there is no doubt that in many instances arrowheads were placed as grave goods, greater attention will have to be paid in future to their precise context in graves'. One wonders how closely his advice has been heeded and whether further examples of death through archery have been missed, not only in Beaker burials subsequently discovered, but also in those discovered by earlier antiquarians and archaeologists.

How, though, are we to interpret this burial? A number of possibilities spring to mind, and perhaps as Aubrey Burl has suggested (*ibid.*: 296), the Archer may

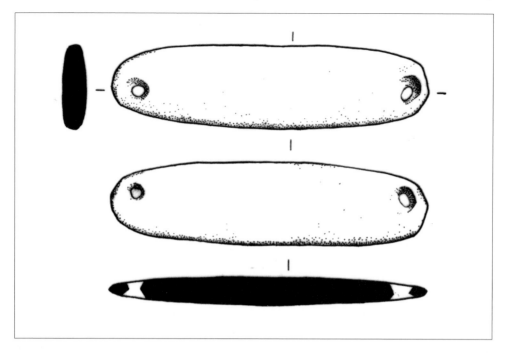

64. Stonehenge Archer's bracer. (Redrawn after Evans)

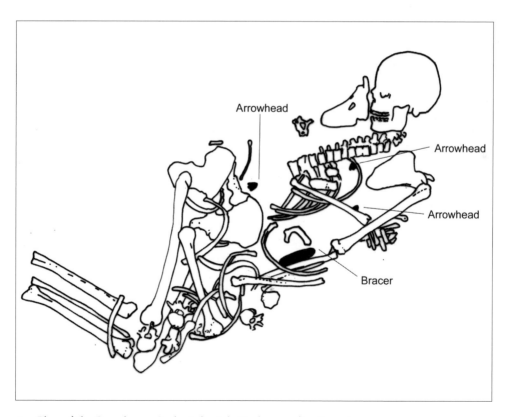

65. Plan of the Stonehenge Archer's burial. (Redrawn after Evans)

have been a stranger who was executed because he had greatly angered local people by somehow desecrating their great religious sanctuary. As Burl (*ibid.*) says, 'it is possible to imagine an unexpected encounter, a panicking flight, the death and burial in the earthwork ditch as an offering to the circle'. Alternatively, it could be that the young man was a war captive who was ritually murdered in honour of the gods – a fate known to have been suffered by many unfortunate people in the ancient world (see Aldhouse Green 2001: 140–143 for examples). Perhaps he was even a common criminal who was executed and buried at the circle as an offering, but Nick Thorpe (2006: 152) has plausibly argued that it is unlikely that a social deviant would be given a burial at such a prestigious site. Perhaps then, the Stonehenge Archer was a renowned warrior who had fought and died bravely on the 'battlefield', and who was thus honoured by being buried at Britain's greatest prehistoric monument?

It could be that a similar story lies behind the cremated remains of the young adult discovered in the centre of the fascinating Sarn-y-bryn-caled timber circle (located near Welshpool in Powys), which forms part of a larger complex of monuments dating from the Late Neolithic to the Early Bronze Age (Gibson 1992, 1994). The circle consisted of an outer and inner ring of substantial oak posts, with the inner ring surrounding a central rectangular pit that contained two cremation burials. The primary burial lay on the base of the pit and it may have originally been contained in a long-since decayed bag or basket. Four high-quality barbed and tanged arrowheads were found amongst the cremated bones, and although they had been turned white or 'calcined' by the heat of the funeral pyre, they had survived almost intact, indicating that the arrowheads had been largely protected from its fierce flames. Alex Gibson (*ibid.*: 155) has therefore credibly suggested 'that they may have been in the body when it was cremated and thus protected from the flame by the flesh'. Further support for the idea that the arrowheads had been the cause of death is provided by the fact that two are missing their points and display clear impact fractures. Although a date obtained on a piece of charcoal from the primary burial suggested a date of death around 2350 BC, further dates obtained from posts of the inner and outer rings came out at *c.* 2100 BC, so there was some uncertainty as to the true date of the burial. However, new dates obtained on the monument and its associated cremation burials indicate that the primary burial was probably inserted within the timber circle in the twenty-first or twentieth century BC (Gibson 2010: 352). It should also be pointed out that Gibson (1992.: 186–187) feels that it is more likely that the person who was very probably killed by the arrowheads is more likely to have been a sacrificial victim, rather than a warfare casualty who may have been given a hero's burial in the centre of the timber circle.

Excavations undertaken at the important prehistoric religious and funerary complex at Barrow Hills, near Radley in Oxfordshire (Barclay & Halpin 1999), have uncovered tantalising signs that this might also have been a place that featured Beaker 'war-graves' containing the 'illustrious dead'. It has to be admitted, however, that the strongest candidate in this respect is Early Bronze Age in date and takes the form of a late Beaker 'flat' grave (Grave 203), which was probably dug in the early centuries of the second millennium BC. The grave contained an adult male (probably aged between twenty and thirty) accompanied by various artefacts including a fine Southern-style Beaker, a bronze awl and six barbed and tanged arrowheads. One of the arrowheads lay next to the man's spine (plate 23) and this almost certainly caused his death. It is perhaps possible that the arrowhead was a grave good, but its position in the grave, and the fact that it had broken barbs and an impact fracture on its tip, argues strongly against this. Although less certainly the cause of death, an arrowhead with a broken barb and slight damage to its tip was found next to the right thigh bone of an adult male (forty to forty-five years of age – old for the standards of the time) who was buried in grave 4660 (dated to 2190–1890 BC). Two arrowheads with damaged tips were also recovered from the grave fill just above the central burial in Barrow 4A (as mentioned in Chapter 1, this may have contained an early Beaker immigrant) and a further arrowhead with damaged tip came from the mound of the barrow. It is quite possible, however, as Alistair Barclay (*ibid.*: 154) has suggested, that these arrows were deposited by those who took place in the funeral rites. A cut mark was identified on the clavicle of the adult male who might have been buried in a 'tree-trunk' coffin in grave 950 (2300–1970 BC), and it could be tentatively suggested that this might represent an act of violence.

Other possible examples of individuals from Beaker groups who perhaps lost their lives in warfare are known, and include the male (aged twenty-five to thirty years) discovered in a sub-rectangular grave (Grave 61) beneath a barrow featuring several burials at Fordington Farm near Dorchester Age (Bellamy 1991). As well as being buried with cattle bones, a barbed and tanged arrowhead lay suggestively in the lower pelvic area of his skeleton (66), but it has to admitted that we cannot be certain whether it was the cause of death or a grave good. A more likely 'casualty of war' was revealed after re-analysis of skeletal material from the Beaker flat grave cemetery at Staxton in Yorkshire found that one of the men buried in the cemetery had received a fierce blow from a weapon (possibly a battle-axe), which had seriously injured his left shoulder; it is likely that he died as a result of this injury (Leach in Thorpe *ibid.*: 152–153).

In addition the above evidence, individuals who suffered non-lethal traumatic injuries have been identified in several Beaker graves. It is conceivable that some of these were received in combat; and perhaps the most telling in this respect, are the 'parry' fractures seen on the forearms of some individuals (see Thorpe 2006: 151 for examples), which probably occurred as individuals instinctively raised their arms to protect themselves from an armed attacker. It may be interesting to mention that the individual from the Fordington Farm barrow had what appears to be an example of a healed parry fracture on his right forearm (Jenkins 1991: 120), which may suggest that he was no stranger to violence, and thus, was in fact killed by the arrowhead found with him in his grave.

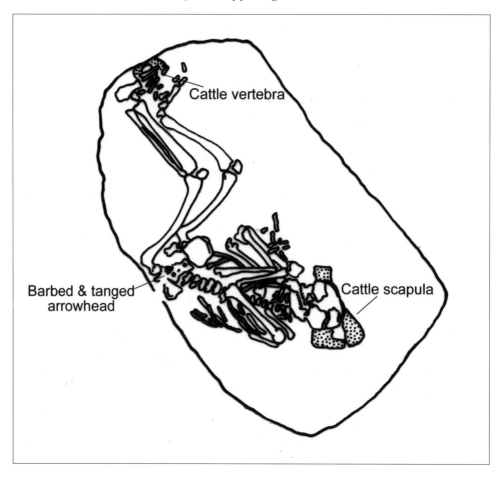

Cattle vertebra

Barbed & tanged
arrowhead

Cattle scapula

66. Plan of Grave 61, Fordington Farm. (Redrawn after Bellamy)

Slight but intriguing evidence, perhaps hinting that Grooved Ware communities also sometimes found themselves embroiled in warfare, either with rival Grooved Ware or Beaker groups, has been found at the Durrington Walls settlement. In a pit cut into the corner of House 547 (which was constructed around 2500 BC), archaeologists discovered a human femur displaying two injuries which are consistent with arrowhead wounds (Mike Parker Pearson pers. comm.).

A Warrior Code?

Although it has to be admitted that there seems to be little sign of Grooved Ware warriors in the British Copper Age (although this does not mean that they did not exist), the story seems to be somewhat different when we turn to archaeological evidence left by Beaker communities. Not only do we have the skeletal evidence pointing towards death and injury in combat, there are also the male Beaker graves containing weaponry, which can be plausibly seen as symbolising the warrior values that emerged in Late Neolithic Europe as a result of the breakdown of the old conservative ways of life during this time (Osgood 2000: 15). Of course, as Richard Osgood (*ibid.*: 16) has rightly pointed out, Beaker graves containing weaponry are often assumed to mark the graves of male warriors, even though the skeletons with which they are found are often not sexed to confirm whether they are male or female. Interestingly, what appear to be female warrior burials have been found in a number of cemeteries belonging to the Nitra culture that occupied parts of Slovakia and Moravia in the second half of the third millennium BC, and which shared many cultural similarities with neighbouring Beaker groups (Hårde 2006). Thus although it is perhaps improbable, we cannot totally rule out the possibility that women were also sometimes active participants in Copper Age warfare in Britain, particularly when it is also considered that there is anthropological evidence revealing that women in stateless societies did sometimes fight alongside men in warfare (see Davie 1929: 32–34).

Perhaps the most obvious expression of the Beaker warrior ethos are the barbed and tanged arrowheads and archers' 'bracers' (as we will see below, many of these objects were probably not used as wrist guards to protect archers' wrists) that are found in Beaker graves throughout Britain (plate 24). Frustratingly, only faint traces of possible bows have been found in British Beaker graves and so it is hard to say for certain what the bows used by Beaker archers looked like. However, some at least, may have been of the short and curved composite type used by several ancient peoples such as the Egyptians or Scythians, as what appear to be miniature representations of such bows, in the form of pendants, have been found in Beaker graves on the Continent (Piggott 1971). Joan Taylor (1994: 47) has also made the interesting suggestion that there was a ranked Beaker archer class, and that the 'knights' who sat at the top of this elite order denoted their status by capping their bracers with gold (plate 24).

Not all, however, have followed this idea of Beaker warrior archers, and for example, Roger Mercer (2006: 128–129), believes that the archery symbolism of the male Beaker graves is more likely to be symbolic of a hunting ritual carried out by members of the Beaker ruling class. Possible evidence that may lend support to Mercer's theory came to light in 1987 during the expansion of Heathrow airport (Cotton *et al.* 2006). Along with many other archaeological discoveries made in the course of this construction work, a large and deep pit (3.10m x 2.15m and *c* .2m deep) containing the remains of an aurochs was uncovered. Six barbed and tanged arrowheads were found in association with the skeletal remains, with four concentrated in the area of the ribs and pelvis (two of these displayed impact fractures), and two lying among the lower leg bones of the animal. As the excavators (*ibid.*: 160) of the aurochs deposit rightly point out, it would be perverse to argue that these arrowheads did not kill the aurochs. It is also likely that its death was not instantaneous, with a combination of blood loss, shock and exhaustion finally bringing this mighty beast to its knees in front of the hunters who killed it. Although a firm date was not obtained for this fascinating snapshot of prehistoric hunting, it seems safe to assume that the aurochs was deposited in the pit at some point either in the Copper Age or Early Bronze Age.

The true role of the Beaker archers will never be fully be resolved, as there is evidence to support both the warrior and hunter theories. However, while not denying that some hunting did take place, like others (e.g. Fokkens *et al.* 2005; Sarauw 2006) I believe that it is more probable that the archery equipment (and other items) found in male Beaker graves indicates that those individuals with whom it was buried, were warriors first and hunters second. In support of this argument, it can be noted that arrowheads with barbs and tangs functioned as specialised war projectiles amongst several stateless societies around the world. For example, in contrast to their hunting arrows, which were without barbs (and thus easier to extract), the war arrows used by the Dani of highland New Guinea were barbed so that they would be difficult to extract from the body. To further enhance the chances of infection (which no doubt was a major cause of death in the warfare of stateless societies) they were daubed with grease (Keeley 1996: 52). With similar deadly logic, the Wintu tribes of California used loosely bound barbed points in warfare, which would easily snap from arrow shafts and lodge in bodies (*ibid.*).

Turning to the bracers or wrist guards, it has been convincingly argued (Fokkens *et al.* 2005) that many were actually not worn in a functional position on the inside of the lower arm (where they would protect against the recoil of the bowstring), but rather, were generally worn on the outer arm in an 'ornamental' position, either held in place by leather or sinew ties, or by attachment to a leather wristlet. However, this does not preclude them from having been worn by Beaker warriors, and their association with barbed and tanged arrowheads (which appear to have been designed with warfare in mind) in graves, indicates that they were a further expression of the martial ideology that seems to have been an important aspect of the Beaker culture.

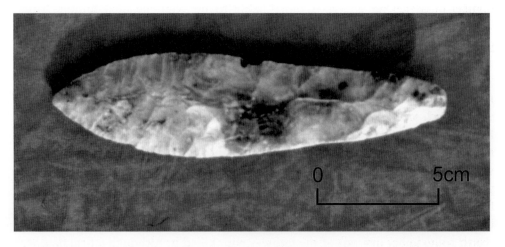

67. Flint dagger from the Isle of Thanet. (Ges Moody/Trust for Thanet Archaeology)

Richard Osgood (2000: 15) has also made the interesting suggestion that Beaker archers may have worn armour (perhaps leather), similar to that depicted in the famous carvings on the Copper Age stelae from Le Petit Chasseur in Switzerland. Quilted or padded costumes can be seen on these anthropomorphic figures and it has been plausibly suggested that they are representations of warriors wearing quilted armour, which provides very good protection against archery, and which has been well recorded in the ethnographic record (*ibid.*: 83).

Further evidence of Copper Age warfare is probably provided by the stone battle-axes that were also introduced into Britain with the arrival of the Beaker culture, but which are first seen on the Continent, in male graves of the Corded Ware culture of Northern Europe. Andrew Sherratt (1997: 192) has said of battle-axes, '[they] are charged with meaning, for they express the ideal of a society whose self-image was not work but warfare'. Although these artefacts could have been used as tools, it appears more likely that they were specifically designed to inflict deadly damage to the human body, and in particular the skull. As Roger Mercer (2006: 133) has pointed out, the heavy weight of the axe is the important thing to consider, as this means that they would have been particularly effective weapons in hand-to-hand combat, being used to deliver crushing blows to an a enemy's head or upper body. Many of the battle-axes (and other axe types) used by Copper Age and Early Bronze Age communities in Wales and England were made from spotted dolerite that was quarried from Carn Menyn and other outcrops in the Preseli Hills (plate 18) (Williams-Thorpe *et al.* 2006). Several battle-axes have been found in Beaker burials in the Stonehenge region and, for example, in the early nineteenth century, William Cunnington found a Preseli battle-axe and six barbed and tanged arrowheads in the Lake cemetery on Salisbury Plain (Burl 1987: 120). These finds provide us with further evidence that the Preseli Hills were viewed as a special place by Copper Age people.

In light of the warfare waged by Beaker warriors, we should perhaps consider the daggers or knives made from metal or flint, that have also been found in a number of Beaker graves (67). In this book, I have preferred to use the term 'knife' when referring to these objects, as I feel it is more probable that they were designed primarily as cutting implements used for various utilitarian (and perhaps also ritual) purposes, rather than as stabbing weapons to be used in close combat. It has been pointed out by several scholars (e.g. Mercer 2006: 124; Skak-Nielsen 2008: 352) that Beaker 'daggers' are often triangular in shape, have rounded points, and sharp cutting edges, which seems to suggest that it is more probable that they were actually 'knives'. However, while the evidence appears to argue against the dagger theory, this does not mean that Beaker knives were not sometimes employed as stabbing weapons in warfare, as they could certainly have caused serious and lethal damage to unprotected parts of the body, even if they were 'one-chance' weapons (Osgood 2000: 23). In fact, although located in Southern France, an individual found in the multiple Beaker burial at Baumes-Chaudes cave had a copper dagger in his thorax, and it may also be worth pointing out that at least seventeen of the 300–400 individuals buried here had arrowhead wounds (Guilaine & Zammit in Vander Linden 2006: 321).

Humphrey Case (in Mercer 2006: 129) has suggested that Beaker archers used their knives to give the *coup de grace* to wounded animals that had been brought down in the hunt, and that the blood of these animals was then drunk from Beakers. It would probably be going a step too far to suggest that Beaker warriors drank the blood of their enemies but it is equally as possible that, in some cases, their knives were used to give the *coup de grace* to humans, as their sharp cutting edges could certainly have been used to 'finish off' seriously wounded enemies who lay on the ground, unable to escape. Some may argue against the idea that Beaker knives were owned by warriors, but whatever one believes about the true identity of their owners, it seems very likely that the metal examples in particular were used as a way of displaying the higher status of the people with which they were buried, as their use seems to have been restricted to a select group.

In addition to the weaponry found in Beaker graves, there are also the 'halberds' (68) of the Copper Age and Early Bronze Age, which have been found in Scotland, Wales, England, and most parts of Europe, although the key centres of production for these striking but somewhat forgotten artefacts were Ireland, Central Europe and south-east Spain (O' Flaherty 1998: 74; Schuhmacher 2002: 263). As Ronan O'Flaherty (1998: 74) tells us, a 'halberd consists of a long, stout blade [of either copper or bronze] with a strong midrib, attached to a shaft of wood, or, in parts of Central Europe to a shaft of metal'. The British and Irish halberds have blades made from copper and it is probable that they originated in Ireland and Britain around 2350/2300 BC and from here, subsequently spread to the rest of the Continent (Schuhmacher 2002: 280–284). However, archaeological opinion is divided as to what role halberds actually played in Copper Age and Early Bronze Age society, *c.* 2300–1800 BC, with one camp favouring the idea that they were non-utilitarian symbols of power, and the other arguing that they were deadly weapons used in hand-to-hand combat. While some halberds (e.g. the metal-shafted types found in Central Europe), are likely to have mainly been used for display, the Irish examples, at least, show clear signs of wear (O'Flaherty 1998: 75). Experiments with a replica Irish Halberd have also revealed that they would be very effective killing weapons, which may well have been used in duels between 'champions' (O'Flaherty 2007).

The Causes of Copper Age Warfare: Some Suggestions

Exactly why warfare broke out Britain's Copper Age communities lies beyond our reach, but it seems safe to assume that there were many reasons why they 'went to war', and one distinct possibility is that people fought over material resources or 'booty'. In particular, cattle might have been a common cause of warfare in Copper Age Britain, as they would have been an important type of mobile wealth that could be quite easily stolen (Christensen 2004: 152). Some support for this idea may be provided by evidence from the ethnographic record, which reveals that in many stateless societies cattle were valuable both in terms of sustenance

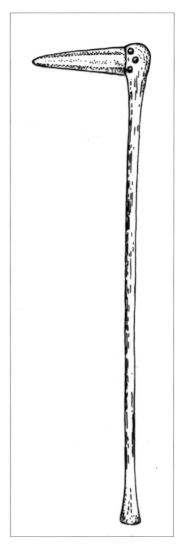

68. Prehistoric halberd. (Author)

and status, and have often been the driving force behind warfare. A great deal of evidence for this cattle-driven warfare has been found in Africa (see Davie 1929: 83–86), with many of its tribal peoples (e.g. the famous Masai and Dinka to name but a few) involved in frequent raiding for bovine booty, or in the many violent reprisals that took place as a result of this cattle theft. There is also evidence from the ancient world attesting to the link between cattle and warfare. For instance, there are Egyptian inscriptions recording that the Hebrews of the Old Testament often sent out raiding parties, which had the principal aim of capturing large quantities of cattle, although other livestock such as sheep and goats were also taken (*ibid.*: 1929: 87). A similar situation existed in Ancient Greece, where cattle raiding was a common cause of warfare and was also seen as a legitimate way of increasing the size of one's herd and wealth, with death during cattle raiding perceived as an honourable way for a warrior to die (*ibid.*).

Sometimes it may not only have been the capture of livestock that motivated Copper Age warfare in Britain, but people too, with attacks made on other groups in order to catch slaves who could be forced to labour for their captors. Such predatory warfare has been observed amongst many societies around the world (e.g. the Chagga of Northern Tanzania, who used natural and artificial caves on the slopes of Kilimanjaro as protection from slave raiding – see Clack 2010) and the procurement of slaves could also be used as a means of enhancing one's status (Mitchell 1984). It should also be pointed out that it was not uncommon for one group to attack another in order to capture women for wives, particularly in stateless societies where polygyny was practised (Davie 1929: 97–102; Clack 2010: 325; Gat 2006: 69–75).

There may also have been other resources that British Copper Age communities fought over, and raw materials such as flint, salt, tin, and copper ore, may have sparked warfare on occasion, with those who had no access to such materials (either because they were controlled by another group, or because they were not found in their territory) perhaps sometimes resorting to armed aggression in order to obtain them. Armed raids may also have been made on enemy settlements with the intention of stealing stored grain, and the actual land that produced this grain could perhaps also have caused warfare to break out. Fertile farmland would have been desirable, because the crops that it produced can be seen as a type of wealth or 'capital', which could be consumed immediately or saved for future use, and thus this wealth could have invited aggression, as its seizure would mean that the burden of working the land was lessened for the aggressors (Davie 1929: 80). Disputes over boundaries or territories could also have spiralled out of control into open warfare, and perhaps some continental Beaker groups arriving in Britain were not always welcomed with open arms by the native communities on whose land they wished to settle.

Another possibility is that Copper Age warfare was sometimes caused by ambitious and ruthless individuals trying to maintain and strengthen positions of power. Such individuals have been observed amongst the tribal peoples of Papua New Guinea, for example, where 'Machiavellian' leaders or 'big men', struggling to maintain their shaky leadership, were often the driving force behind the frequent wars that broke out between different clans (Sillitoe 1978). Although they were unable to directly control or initiate war, big men were able to use their influence to encourage attacks on their rivals in other communities who threatened their hegemony (*ibid.*: 254). Thus it could be that 'big men' of native Grooved Ware groups sometimes initiated warfare because they felt threatened by their Beaker counterparts whose access to novel and exotic goods may have given them an advantage in the power struggles that very probably took place in Copper Age Britain. Alternatively, as has often been the case in both 'primitive' and 'civilised' societies, it may simply have been a lust for more power and wealth that triggered warfare amongst Britain's Copper age communities.

Perhaps it was just fear of being attacked by another community that sometimes ignited warfare in Copper Age Britain? As Azar Gat (2006: 97) has rightly pointed out, the 'other' may be regarded as a potential enemy who might suddenly attack one day and thus one side may decide to resolve this 'security dilemma' by choosing to attack the other in order to seriously weaken or eliminate them (*ibid*.: 99). It should be pointed out, however, that in contrast to other periods of British prehistory, many archaeologists believe that there is no clear evidence to show that signs that Britain's Copper Age communities took measures to combat the threat of attack by fortifying their sites and settlements. However, a notable dissenter against this view is Aubrey Burl (1991: 42), who has argued that the 'super-henges' of southern England (i.e. Avebury, Durrington Walls, Marden, Mount Pleasant and Knowlton) and other comparable sites elsewhere in Britain, were actually fortified settlements that were protected from attack by massive banks and ditches. Burl certainly finds himself in a minority with his theory, but perhaps archaeologists all too easily dismiss the idea that some of the huge earthwork enclosures that were in use from the Late Neolithic to the Early Bronze Age, were in fact, defensive in nature. In fact, at the Mount Pleasant henge in Dorset at least, there is tantalising evidence to suggest that Burl could well be right, and which perhaps also points to an actual outbreak of warfare. During his famous excavations at the site, Geoffrey Wainwright discovered that around 2100 BC, people had constructed a massive palisade consisting of around 1,600 timber posts, which reached about 6m in height (Pitts 2000: 68). Mike Pitts (*ibid*.) has argued that this massive timber palisade was clearly military in character and, furthermore, its builders used the hill's contours to enhance its defensive potential. Intriguingly, Wainwright's investigations at the site also revealed that shortly after its construction, the palisade was deliberately set on fire and its posts uprooted (*ibid*.: 292).

Nick Thorpe (2000: 12) has plausibly suggested that warfare amongst prehistoric hunter-gatherer communities 'arose over matters of personal honour – such as slights, insults, marriages going wrong, or theft'. As Thorpe (*ibid*.) further says, '[i]n a small hunter-gatherer community, everyone is related. An attack on one group member is an attack on the whole family. A personal feud may quickly involve the whole community. From there it is a small step to war'. Although Britain's Copper Age communities were not hunter-gatherers but agriculturalists, in many cases they probably also consisted of kin-based groups and it is equally possible that warfare also occurred amongst them for similar reasons.

It may also have been the case that warfare in Copper Age Britain was sometimes driven by individuals seeking status and prestige. As John Kennedy (1971: 45) has pointed out, 'one of the most common motivations found in the war patterns of primitive societies is the association of ego-validation with manhood and valour. Along with this goes the assignment of at least some prestige and power to the successful warrior'. Azar Gat (2006: 89) has argued that '[i]n traditional societies … [w]here no strong centralized authority existed, one's honour was a social commodity of vital significance, affecting both somatic and reproductive chances'. In other words, by acquiring greater status and prestige through warfare, warriors thus enhanced their chances of obtaining both resources and women.

Whatever motivated warfare in Copper Age Britain, we must not lose sight of the fact that although the archaeological evidence from this period reveals the existence of an innovative, intelligent, and highly skilled society, capable of producing remarkable monuments and beautiful objects, sadly, it also shows warfare had some role to play in this society. Whether this was a major or minor role remains a matter of debate, and its true significance will remain with the long-vanished people who lived and died during one of the most exciting and intriguing chapters in the story of Britain.

BIBLIOGRAPHY

Adams, W. Y., Van Gerven, D. P. & Levy, R. S. 1978. 'The Retreat From Migrationism', *Annual Review of Anthropology* 7: 483–532.

Aldhouse-Green, M. 2001. *Dying for the Gods: Human Sacrifice in Iron Age and Roman Europe*. Stroud: Tempus.

Allen, M. J. 2005. 'Beaker Settlement and Environment on the Chalk Downs of Southern England', *Proceedings of the Prehistoric Society* 71: 219–245.

Anthony, D. 1990. Migration in Archaeology: The Baby and the Bathwater, *American Anthropologist* 92: 895–914.

Anthony, D. 1997. 'Prehistoric Migration as Social Process', in J. Chapman & H. Hamerow (eds) *Migrations and Invasions in Archaeological Explanation*. Oxford: British Archaeological Reports (International Series) 664: 21–33.

Arcà, A. 2004. 'The topographic engravings of Alpine rock art: fields, settlements and agricultural landscapes', in C. Chippindale & G. Nash (eds) *Pictures in Place: The Figured Landscapes of Rock-Art*. Cambridge: Cambridge University Press: 318–349.

Armit, I. 1996. *The Archaeology of Skye and the Western Isles*. Edinburgh: Edinburgh University Press.

Arsenault, D. 2004a. 'From natural settings to spiritual places in the Algonkian sacred landscape: an archaeological, ethnohistorical and ethnographic analysis of Canadian Shield rock art sites', in C. Chippindale & G. Nash (eds) *Pictures in Place: The Figured Landscapes of Rock-Art*. Cambridge: Cambridge University Press: 289–317.

Arsenault, D. 2004b. 'Rock-art, landscape, sacred places: attitudes in contemporary archaeological theory', in C. Chippindale & G. Nash (eds) *Pictures in Place: The Figured Landscapes of Rock-Art*. Cambridge: Cambridge University Press: 69–84.

Ashmore, P. J. 1986. 'Neolithic carvings in Maes Howe', *Proceedings of the Society of Antiquaries of Scotland* 116: 57–62.

Ashmore, P. J. 1989. 'Excavation of a Beaker cist at Dornoch Nursery, Sutherland', *Proceedings of the Society of Antiquaries of Scotland* 119: 63–71.

Ashmore, P. J. 1996. *Neolithic and Bronze Age Scotland*. London: B. T. Batsford/ Historic Scotland.

Asombang, R. N. 2004. 'Interpreting standing stones in Africa: a case study in north-west Cameroon', *Antiquity* 300: 294–305.

Atkinson, R. J. C. 1967. 'Silbury Hill', *Antiquity* XLI: 259–262.

Bahn, P. 2009. 'Shammanism: A Dead End in Rock-Art Studies', in Beckensall, S. 2009. *Prehistoric Rock Art in Britain*. Stroud: Amberley. Appendix VIII: 150–153.

Barber, B. 1941. 'A Socio-Cultural Interpretation of the Peyote Cult', *American Anthropologist* 43: 673–675.

Barber, M. 2003. *Bronze and the Bronze Age: Metalwork and Society in Britain c. 2500 – 800 BC*. Stroud: Tempus.

Barber, M. 2005. 'Mining, Burial and Chronolgy: the West Sussex Flint Mines in the Late Neolithic and Early Bronze Age', in P. Topping & M. Lynott (eds) *The Cultural Landscape of Prehistoric Mines*. Oxford: Oxbow: 94–109.

Barclay, A. 1999. 'Grooved Ware from the Upper Thames Region', in R. Cleal & A. MacSween (eds) *Grooved Ware in Britain and Ireland (Neolithic Studies Group Seminar Papers 3)*. Oxford: Oxbow: 9–22.

Barclay, A. 2010. 'Excavating the Living Dead', *British Archaeology* 115: 36–41.

Barclay, G. & Halpin, C. 1999. *Excavations at Barrow Hills, Radley, Oxfordshire. Volume 1: The Neolithic and Bronze Age Monument Complex*. Oxford: Oxford Archaeological Unit.

Barclay, G. J. & Russell-White, C. J. (eds) 1993. 'Excavations in the ceremonial complex of the fourth to second millennium BC at Balfarg/Balbirnie, Glenrothes, Fife', *Proceedings of the Society of Antiquaries of Scotland* 123: 43–210.

Barrett, J. C. 1990. 'The Monumentality of Death: The Character of Early Bronze Age Mortuary Mounds in Southern Britain', *World Archaeology* 22: 179–189.

Barrett, J. C. & Fewster, K. J. 1998. 'Stonehenge: *is* the medium the message?' *Antiquity* 72: 847–852.

Bates, B. 2003. *The Real Middle Earth: Magic and Mystery in the Dark Ages*. London: Pan.

Bayliss, A., McAvoy, F. & Whittle, A. 2007. 'The world recreated: redating Silbury Hill in its monumental landscape', *Antiquity* 81: 26–53.

Beckensall, S. 1983. *Northumberland's Prehistoric Rock Carvings*. Rothbury: Pendulum.

Beckensall, S. 2009. *Prehistoric Rock Art in Britain*. Stroud: Amberley.

Bellamy. P. S. 1991. 'The Excavation of Fordington Farm Round Barrow'. *Proceedings of the Dorset Natural History and Archaeological Society* 113: 107–132.

Bender, B. 1992. 'Theorising Landscapes and the Prehistoric Landscapes of Stonehenge', *Man* 27: 735–755.

Bevins, R. E., Pearce, N. J. G. & Ixer, R. A. 2011. 'Stonehenge rhyolitic bluestone sources and the application of zircon chemistry as a new tool for provenancing rhyalitic lithics', *Journal of Archaeological Science* 38: 605–622.

Binford, L. 1962. 'Archaeology as Anthropology', *American Antiquity* 28: 217–225.

Bewley, R. 2003. *Prehistoric Settlements*. Stroud: Tempus.

Boyd, C. E. & Dering, J. P. 1996. 'Medicinal and hallucinogenic plants identified in the sediments and pictographs of the Lower Pecos, Texas Archaic', *Antiquity* 268: 256–275.

Bradley, R. 1970. 'The Excavation of a Beaker Settlement at Belle Tout, East Sussex, England', *Proceedings of the Prehistoric Society* XXXVI: 312–380.

Bradley, R. 1972. 'Prehistorians and Pastoralists in Neolithic and Bronze Age England', *World Archaeology* 4: 192–204.

Bradley, R. 1982. 'Position and Possession: Assemblage Variation in the British Neolithic', *Oxford Journal of Archaeology* 1: 27–38.

Bradley, R. 1991. 'Rock Art and the Perception of Landscape', *Cambridge Archaeological Journal* 1: 77–101.

Bradley, R. 1992. 'Turning the World – Rock-carvings and the Archaeology of Death', in N. Sharples & S. Sheridan (eds). 1992. *Vessels for the Ancestors: Essays on the Neolithic of Britain and Ireland in honour of Audrey Henshall.* Edinburgh: Edinburgh University Press: 168–176.

Bradley, R. 1998. *The Passage of Arms: An archaeological analysis of prehistoric hoard and votive deposits.* Oxford: Oxbow.

Bradley, R. 2002a. 'The land, the sky and the Scottish stone circle', in C. Scarre (ed.) *Monuments and Landscape in Atlantic Europe: Perception and Society during the Neolithic and Early Bronze Age.* London: Routledge: 122–138.

Bradley, R. 20002b. 'Access, Style and Imagery: The Audience for Prehistoric Rock Art in Atlantic Spain and Portugal, 4000–2000 BC', *Oxford Journal of Archaeology* 21: 231–247.

Bradley, R. 2007. *The Prehistory of Britain and Ireland.* Cambridge: Cambridge University Press.

Bradley, R. 2009. *Image and Audience: Rethinking Prehistoric Art.* Oxford: Oxford University Press.

Bradley, R. & Fábregas Valcarce, R. 1998. 'Crossing the Border: Contrasting Styles of Rock Art in the Prehistory of North-West Iberia', *Oxford Journal of Archaeology* 17: 287–308.

Brindley, A. L. 2004. 'Prehistoric Pottery', in W. O'Brien (ed.) *Ross Island: Mining, Metal and Society in Early Ireland.* Galway: National University of Ireland Department of Archaeology Bronze Age Studies 6: 316–337.

British Archaeology Magazine 2010 (115). *Britain in Archaeology: Ness of Brodgar*: 8–9.

Brodie, N. 1994. *The Neolithic – Bronze Age Transition in Britain: A critical review of some archaeological and craniological concepts*, Oxford: British Archaeological Reports (British Series) 238.

Brodie, N. 1997. 'New Perspectives on the Bell-Beaker Culture', *Oxford Journal of Archaeology* 16: 297–314.

Brodie, N. 1998. 'British Bell Beakers: Twenty-five years of theory and practice', in M. Benz & S. van Willigen (eds) *Some New Approaches to the Bell Beaker Phenomenon: Lost Paradise...?* Oxford: British Archaeological Reports (International Series) 690: 43–57.

Bruce, J. R, Megaw, E. M. & Megaw, B. R. S. 1947. 'A Neolithic site at Ronaldsway, Isle of Man', *Proceedings of the Prehistoric Society* XIII: 139–160.

Brück, J. 2004. 'Material metaphors: The relational construction of identity in Early Bronze Age burials in Britain and Ireland', *Journal of Social Archaeology* 4: 307–333.

Budd, P. 2000. 'Meet the Metal Makers', *British Archaeology* 56: 12–17.

Budd, P., Gale, D., Pollard, A. M., Thomas, R. G. & Williams, P. A. 1992. 'The early development of metallurgy in the British Isles', *Antiquity* 66: 677–686.

Budd, P. & Taylor, T. 1995. 'The faerie smith meets the bronze industry: magic versus science in the interpretation of prehistoric metal-making', *World Archaeology* 27: 133–143.

Burl, A. 1976. *The Stone Circles of the British Isles*, London: Yale University Press.

Burl, A. 1969–70. 'The Recumbent Stone Circles of North-East Scotland', *Proceedings of the Society of Antiquaries of Scotland* 102: 56–81.

Burl, A. 1981. *Rites of the Gods*, London: J. M. Dent.

Burl, A. 1987. *The Stonehenge People*, London: J. M. Dent.

Burl, A. 1988. *Four-Posters: Bronze Age Stone Circles of Western Europe*. British Archaeological Reports 195.

Burl, A. 1991. *Prehistoric Henges*, Shire: Princes Risborough.

Burl, A. 1997. *Prehistoric Astronomy and Ritual*, Shire: Princes Risborough.

Burl, A. 1999. *Circles of Stone: The Prehistoric Rings of Britain and Ireland*, London: Harvill.

Burl, A. 2005. *Prehistoric Stone Circles*, Shire: Princes Risborough.

Burl, A. 2007: *A Brief History of Stonehenge: A Complete History and Archaeology of the World's Most Enigmatic Stone Circle*, London: Robinson.

Burmeister, S. 2000. 'Archaeology and Migration: Approaches to an Archaeological Proof of Migration', *Current Anthropology* 41: 539–567.

Burrow, S. 1997. *The Neolithic Culture of the Isle of Man: A study of the sites and pottery*, British Archaeological Reports (British Series) 263.

Burrow, S. & Darvill, T. 1997. 'AMS Dating of the Manx Ronaldsway Culture', *Antiquity* 71: 412–419.

Calder, C. S. 1949–50. 'Report on the excavation of a Neolithic Temple at Stanydale in the parish of Sandsting, Shetland', *Proceedings of the Society of Antiquaries of Scotland* 84: 185–205.

Calder, C. S. T. 1955–56. 'Report on the Discovery of Numerous Stone Age House-Sites in Shetland', *Proceedings of the Society of Antiquaries of Scotland* 89: 340–397.

Callander, J. G. 1930–31. 'Notes on (1) Certain Prehistoric relics from Orkney, and (2) Skara Brae: its Culture and its Period', *Proceedings of the Society of Antiquaries of Scotland* 65: 78–103.

Campbell, M., Scott, J. G. & Piggott, S. 1960–61. 'The Badden cist slab', *Proceedings of the Society of Antiquaries of Scotland* 94: 46–61.

Carman, J. & Harding, A. (eds) 1999. *Ancient Warfare*. Stroud: Sutton.

Case, H. 1993. 'Beakers: deconstruction and after', *Proceedings of the Prehistoric Society* 59: 241–268.

Case, H. 1997. 'Stonehenge Revisited', *The Wiltshire Archaeological and Natural History Magazine*: 161–168.

Case, H. 2007. 'Beakers and the Beaker Culture', in C. Burgess, P. Topping & F. Lynch (eds) *Beyond Stonehenge: Essays on the Bronze Age in Honour of Colin Burgess*. Oxford: Oxbow: 237–255.

Catling, C. 2007. 'Message in the Stones', *Current Archaeology* 212: 12–19.

Catling, C. 2009. 'Bluestonehenge', *Current Archaeology* 237: 22–28.

Catling, C. 2010. 'Magic & Mining: the Alderley Edge Landscape Project', *Current Archaeology* 238: 22–31.

Chadburn, A., McAvoy, F., Campbell, G., 2005. 'A Green Hill Long Ago: Inside the hill', *British Archaeology* 80: 12–19.

Chadwick, A. & Pollard, J. 2005. 'A Ring cairn and Beaker Burial at Gray Hill, Llanfair Discoed, Monmouthshire', *Past* 50: 11–14.

Chambon, P. 2004. *Collective graves in France during the Bell Beaker phenomenon. In Graves and Funerary Rituals during the Late Neolithic and the Early Bronze Age in Europe (2700–2000 BC)*, Oxford: British Archaeological Reports (International Series) 1284: 69–79.

Chapman, J. 1997. 'The Impact of Modern Invasions and Migrations on Archaeological Explanation', in J. Chapman & H. Hamerow (eds) *Migrations and Invasions in Archaeological Explanation*. Oxford: British Archaeological Reports (International Series) 664: 11–21.

Childe, V. G. 1929a. *The Danube in Prehistory*. Oxford: Clarendon Press.

Childe, V. G. 1941. 'War in Prehistoric Societies', *Sociological Review* 33: 126–138.

Childe, V. G. 1929–30. 'Operations at Skara Brae during 1929–1930', *Proceedings of the Society of Antiquaries of Scotland* 64: 158–191.

Childe, V. G. & Grant, W. G. 1938. 'A Stone-Age Settlement at the Braes of Rinyo, Rousay, Orkney', *Proceedings of the Society of Antiquaries of Scotland* 73: 6–31.

Childe. V. G. & Paterson, J. W. 1928–29. 'Provisional Report on the Excavations at Skara Brae and on Finds from the 1927 & 1928 Campaigns', *Proceedings of the Society of Antiquaries of Scotland* 63: 225–280.

Childe, V. G. 1930–31. 'Final Report on the Operations at Skara Brae', *Proceedings of the Society of Antiquaries of Scotland* 65: 27–77.

Chippindale, C. & Nash, G. 2004. 'Pictures in place: approaches to the figured landscapes of rock art', in C. Chippendale & G. Nash (eds) *Pictures in Place: Figured Landscapes of Rock-art*. Cambridge: Cambridge University Press: 1–36.

Christensen, J. 2004. 'Warfare in the European Neolithic', *Acta Archaeologica* 75: 129–156.

Clack, T. 2009. 'Sheltering experience in underground places: thinking through precolonial Chagga caves on Mount Kilimanjaro', *World Archaeology* 41: 321–344.

Clark, C. P. & Martin, S. R. 2005. 'A Risky Business: Late Woodland Copper Mining on Lake Superior', in P. Topping & M. Lynott (eds) *The Cultural Landscape of Prehistoric Mines*. Oxford: Oxbow. 110–123.

Clarke, D. 1973. 'Archaeology: the loss of innocence', *Antiquity* XLVII: 6–18.

Clarke, D. L. 1970. *Beaker Pottery of Great Britain and Ireland*. Cambridge: Cambridge University Press.

Clarke, D. V., Ritchie, A. & Ritchie, G. 1984. 'Two cists from Boatbridge Quarry, Thankerton, Lanarkshire'. *Proceedings of the Royal Society of Antiquaries of Scotland* 114: 557–588.

Clarke, D. V. & Sharples, N. 1985 in C. Renfrew (ed.) *The Prehistory of Orkney*. Edinburgh: Edinburgh University Press, 54–82.

Clark, G. 1966. 'The Invasion Hypothesis in British Archaeology', *Antiquity* XL: 172–189.

Clark, G. J. D. 1931. 'The Dual Character of the Beaker Invasion', *Antiquity* XX: 415–426.

Cleal, R. 1988. 'The Occurrence of Drilled Holes in Later Neolithic pottery', *Oxford Journal of Archaeology* 7: 139–145.

Cleal, R. 1999. 'Introduction: The What, Where, When and Why of Grooved Ware', in R. Cleal & A. MacSween (eds) *Grooved Ware in Britain and Ireland (Neolithic Studies Group Seminar Papers 3)*. Oxford: Oxbow: 1–8.

Cook, M., Ellis, C. & Sheridan, A. 2010. 'Excavations at Upper Largie Quarry, Argyll & Bute, Scotland: New Light on the Prehistoric Ritual Landscape of the Kilmartin Glen', *Proceedings of the Prehistoric Society* 76: 165–212.

Cooper, L. & Hunt, L. 2005. 'An Engraved Neolithic Plaque with Grooved Ware Associations', *Past* 50: 14–15.

Cotton, J., Elsden, N., Pipe, A. & Rayner, L. 2006. 'Taming the Wild: A Final Neolithic/Earlier Bronze Age Aurochs Deposit from West London', in D. Serjeanston & D. Field (eds) *Animals in the Neolithic of Britain and Europe (Neolithic Studies Group Seminar Papers 7)*. Oxford: Oxbow: 149–167.

Cree, J. E. 1908. 'Notice of a prehistoric kitchen midden and superimposed medieval stone floor found at Tusculum, North Berwick', *Proceedings of the Royal Society of Antiquaries of Scotland* XLII: 253–294.

Current Archaeology Magazine 2007 (208). *Before Stonehenge: village of wild parties*: 17–21.

Current Archaeology Magazine 2010 (247). *News: Excavating the Marden Superhenge*: 6–7.

Current Archaeology Magazine 2011 (251). *Digging a Dolmen: Recent excavations at Trefael, Pembrokeshire*: 40–41.

Curtis, N. 2010. 'The Moon, The Bonfire and the Beaker? Analysing White Inlay from Beaker Pottery in Aberdeenshire', *Past* 65: 1–3.

Curwen, E. C. 1954. *The Archaeology of Sussex*. London: Methuen.

Dark, K. R. 1995. *Theoretical Archaeology*. London: Duckworth.

Darvill, T. 2007. *Stonehenge: The Biography of a Landscape*. Stroud: Tempus.

Darvill, T. & O'Connor, B. 2005. 'The Cronk yn How Stone and the Rock Art of the Isle of Man', *Proceedings of the Prehistoric Society* 71: 283–331.

Darvill, T. & Wainwright, G. 2002. 'Spaces – exploring Neolithic landscapes in south-west Wales and beyond', *Antiquity* 76: 623–624.

Darvill, T. & Wainwright, G. 2003. 'Stone circles, oval settings and henges in south-west Wales and beyond', *Antiquaries Journal* 83: 9–46.

Darvill, T. & Wainwright, G. 2011. 'The Stones of Stonehenge: Revealing secrets from the sacred circle', *Current Archaeology* 252: 28–35.

David, N., Sterner, J. & Gavua, K. 1988. 'Why Pots are Decorated', *Current Anthropology* 29: 365–389.

Davidson, C. B. 1869. 'Notice of further stone kists found at Broomend near the Inverurie Paper-Mills', *Proceedings of the Royal Society of Antiquaries of Scotland* VII: 115–118.

Davie, M. R. 1929. *The Evolution of War: A Study of its Role in Early Societies*. New Haven: Yale University Press.

Davis, S. & Payne, S. 1993. 'A barrow full of cattle skulls', *Antiquity* 67: 12–22.

Deacon, J. 1988. 'The power of a place in understanding southern San rock engravings', *World Archaeology* 20: 129–140.

De Sélincourt (trans.), A. 1972. *Herodotus: The Histories*. London: Penguin.

Diáz-Andreu, M. 2003. 'Rock Art and Ritual Landscapes in Central Spain: The Rock Carvings of La Hinojosa', *Oxford Journal of Archaeology* 22: 35–51.

Dickins, J. 1996. 'A remote analogy?: from Central Australian tjurunga to Irish Early Bronze Age axes', *Antiquity* 70: 161–167.

Dickson, J. H. 1978. 'Bronze Age Mead', *Antiquity* 52: 108–113.

Dineley, M. 2004. *Barley, Malt and Ale in the Neolithic*. British Archaeological Reports (International Series) 1213.

Dobkin de Rios, M. 1986. 'Enigma of Drug-Induced States of Consciousness Among the Kung Bushmen of the Kalahari Desert', *Journal of Ethnopharmacology* 15: 297–304.

Donaldson, P. 1977. 'The excavation of a multiple round barrow at Barnack, Cambridgeshire', *Antiquaries Journal* 57: 197–231.

Douglas Price, T., Grupe, G. & Schröter, P. 1998. 'Migration in the Bell Beaker period of Central Europe', *Antiquity* 72: 405–411.

Douglas Price, T., Knipper, C., Grupe, G. & Smrcka, V. 2004. 'Strontium Isotopes and Prehistoric Migration: The Bell Beaker Period in Central Europe', *European Journal of Archaeology* 7: 9–40.

Dowson, T. A. 'Writing History: Rock Art and Social Change in Southern Africa', *World Archaeology* 25: 332–345.

Dronfield, J. 1995: 'Migraine, Light and Hallucinogens: The Neurocognitive Basis of Irish Megalithic Art', *Oxford Journal of Archaeology* 14: 261–275.

Dudd, N. & Evershed, R. P. & Gibson, A. M. 1999. 'Evidence for Varying Patterns of Exploitation of Animal Products in Different Prehistoric Pottery Traditions Based on Lipids Preserved in Surface and Absorbed Residues', *Journal of Archaeological Science* 26: 1473–1482.

Edmonds, M. 1992. 'Their Use is Wholly Unknown', in N. Sharples & S. Sheridan (eds) *Vessels for the Ancestors: Essays on the Neolithic of Britain and Ireland in honour of Audrey Henshall*. Edinburgh: Edinburgh University Press. 168–176.

Edmonds, M. 1995. *Stone Tools and Society: Working Stone in Neolithic and Bronze age Britain*. London: B. T. Batsford.

Eliade, M. 1978. *The Forge and the Crucible*. Chicago: The University of Chicago Press.

Ericson, J. E. 1985. 'Strontium Isotope Characterization in the Study of Prehistoric Human Ecology', *Journal of Human Evolution* 14: 503–514.

Evans, D. C. 2006. 'An Engraved Neolithic Plaque and Associated Finds from King's Stanley, Gloucestershire', *Past* 52: 3–5.

Evans, D. C. 2010. 'Two Neolithic Pits at King's Stanley, Gloucestershire', *Transactions of the Bristol and Gloucestershire Archaeological Society* 128: 29–54.

Evans, J. A., Chenery, C. A. & Fitzpatrick, A. 2006. 'Bronze Age childhood migration of individuals near Stonehenge, revealed by strontium and isotope tooth enamel analysis', *Archaeometry* 48: 309–322.

Evans, J. G. 1984. 'The Environment in the Late Neolithic and early Bronze Age *and* a Beaker-Age Burial', *The Wiltshire Archaeological and Natural History Magazine* 78: 7–30.

Fitzpatrick, A. 2002. '"The Amesbury Archer": a well-furnished Early Bronze Age burial in southern England', *Antiquity* 76: 629–30.

Fitzpatrick, A. 2003. 'The Amesbury Archer', *Current Archaeology* 184: 146–152.

Fitzpatrick, A. 2004. 'The Boscombe Bowmen: Builders of Stonehenge?', *Current Archaeology* 193: 10–16.

Fitzpatrick, A. 2004. 'A Sacred Circle on Boscombe Down', *Current Archaeology* 195: 106–107.

Fitzpatrick, A. 2009. 'In his hands and in his head: The Amesbury Archer as a metalworker', in P. Clark (ed.) *Bronze Age Connections: Cultural Contact in Prehistoric Europe*. Oxford: Oxbow. 176–188.

Fokkens, H., Achterkamp, Y. & Kuijpers, M. 2008. 'Bracers or Bracelets? About the Functionality and Meaning of Bell-Beaker Wristguards', *Proceedings of the Prehistoric Society* 74: 109–140.

Forde-Johnston, J. L. 1957. 'Megalithic Art in the North-West of Britain: The Calderstones, Liverpool', *Proceedings of the Prehistoric Society* 23: 20–39.

Fox, C. 1942. 'A Beaker Barrow, Enlarged in the Middle Bronze Age, at South Hill, Talbenny, Pembrokeshire', *Archaeological Journal* 99: 1–32.

Garnham, T. 2004. *Lines on the Landscape Circles from the Sky*. Stroud: Tempus.

Garrido, P. R. 1997. 'Bell Beakers in the Southern Meseta of the Iberian Peninsula: Socioeconomic Context and New Data', *Oxford Journal of Archaeology* 16: 187–209.

Garwood, P. 1999. 'Radiocarbon Dating and the Chronology of the Monument Complex', in A. Barclay & C. Halpin (eds) *Excavation at Barrow Hills, Radley, Oxfordshire. Volume 1: The Neolithic and Bronze Age Monument Complex*. Oxford: Oxford Archaeological Unit: 293–309.

Gat. A. 1999. 'The Pattern of Fighting in Simple, Small-Scale, Prestate Societies', *Journal of Anthropological Research* 55: 563–583.

Gibson, A. 1980. 'Pot beakers in Britain?' *Antiquity* 212: 219–221.

Gibson, A. 1986. 'Neolithic and Early Bronze Age Pottery'. Princes Risborough: Shire.

Gibson, A. 1992. 'The timber circle at Sarn-y-bryn-caled, Welshpool, Powys. Ritual and sacrifice in Bronze Age mid-Wales', *Antiquity* 66: 84–92.

Gibson, A. 1994. 'Excavations at the Sarn-y-bryn-caled Cursus Complex, Welshpool, Powys', *Proceedings of the Prehistoric Society* 60: 143–217.

Gibson, A. 2002. *Prehistoric Pottery in Britain & Ireland*. Stroud: Tempus.

Gibson, A. 2005. *Stonehenge and Timber Circles*. Stroud: Tempus.

Gibson, A. 2010. 'New dates for Sarn-y-bryn-caled, Powys, Wales', *Proceedings of the Prehistoric Society* 76: 351–356.

Gillings, M. & Pollard, J. 1999. 'Non-Portable Stone Artifacts and Contexts of Meaning: The Tale of Grey Wether' (www.museums.ncl.ac.uk/Avebury/stone4.htm) *World Archaeology* 31: 179–193.

Gillings, M. & Pollard, J. 2004. *Avebury*. London: Duckworth.

Godwin, H. 1967. 'The Ancient Cultivation of Hemp', *Antiquity* XLI: 42–49.

Gosselain, O.P. 1992. 'Technology and Style: Potters and Pottery Among Bafia of Cameroon', *Man* 27: 559–586.

Green, C. & Rollo-Smith, S. 1984. 'The Excavation of Eighteen Round Barrows near Shrewton, Wiltshire', *Proceedings of the Prehistoric Society* 50: 255–318.

Griffiths, W. E. 1957. 'The Typology & Origins of Beakers in Wales', *Proceedings of the Prehistoric Society* XXIII: 57–90.

Grøn, O. & Kosko, M. M. 2007. 'Stonhenge – Olenok, Siberia: universals or different phenomena? Ethnoarchaeological observations of a midsummer rite', in M. Larsson and M. Parker Pearson (eds) *From Stonehenge to the Baltic: Living with cultural diversity in the third millennium BC*. British Archaeological Reports (International Series) 1692: 175–182.

Grupe, G., Douglas Price, T., Schröter, P., Söllner, F., Johnson, C. M. & Beard, B. L. 1997. 'Mobility of Bell Beaker people revealed by strontium isotope ratios of tooth and bone: a study of southern Bavarian skeletal remains', *Applied Geochemistry* 12: 517–525.

Guerra-Doce, E. 2006. 'Exploring the Significance of Beaker Pottery through Residue Analysis', *World Archaeology*: 247–259.

Haggarty, A. 1991. 'Macrie Moor, Arran: recent excavations at two stone circles', *Proceedings of the Society of Antiquaries of Scotland* 121: 51–94.

Hamerow, H. 2007. 'Migration Theory and the Anglo-Saxon "Identity Crisis"', in J. Chapman & H. Hamerow (eds) *Migrations and Invasions in Archaeological Explanation*. Oxford: British Archaeological Reports (International Series) 664: 33–45.

Hårde. A. 2006. 'Funerary Rituals and Warfare in the Early Bronze Age Nitra Culture of Slovakia and Moravia', in T. Otto, H. Thrane & H. Vankilde (eds) *Warfare and Society: Archaeological and Social Anthropological Perspectives*. Aarhus: Aarhus University Press: 341–391.

Harding, J. 2003. *Henge Monuments of the British Isles*. Stroud: Tempus.

Harding, J. 2006. 'Pit-Digging, Occupation and Structured Deposition on Rudston Wold, Eastern Yorkshire', *Oxford Journal of Archaeology* 25: 109–126.

Harding, P. 1988. 'The Chalk Plaque Pit, Amesbury', *Proceedings of the Prehistoric Society* 54: 320–326.

Harrison, R. J. 1974. 'Origins of the Bell Beaker cultures', *Antiquity* XLVIII: 99–109.

Harrison, R. J. 1980. *The Beaker Folk: Copper Age Archaeology in Western Europe*. London: Thames & Hudson.

Harrison, R. J., Jackson, R. & Napthan, M. 1999. 'A Rich Bell Beaker Burial from Wellington Quarry, Marden, Herefordshire', *Oxford Journal of Archaeology* 18: 1–16.

Harrison, R., Quero, S. & Carmen Priego, M. 1975. 'Beaker Metallurgy in Spain', *Antiquity* XLIX: 273–278.

Healy, F. 2009. 'Wider contacts: Early metalworking and its implications', in A. Barclay & C. Halpin (eds) *Excavations at Barrow Hills, Radley, Oxfordshire. Volume 1: The Neolithic and Bronze Age Monument Complex*. Oxford: Oxford Archaeological Unit: 327–329.

Heath, J. 2009. *Warfare in Prehistoric Britain*. Stroud: Amberley.

Hedges, R. E. M., Houseley, R. A., Bronk Ramsey, C. & Van Klinken, G. J. 1993. 'Radiocarbon Dates from the Oxford AMS System: *Archaeometry* Datelist 17', *Archaeometry* 35: 305–326.

Henshall, A. S. 1955–56. 'Pottery and Stone Implements from Ness of Gruting', in C. S. T. Calder Report on the Discovery of Numerous Stone Age House-Sites in Shetland. *Proceedings of the Society of Antiquaries of Scotland* 89: 381–397.

Henshall, A. S. 1963–64. 'A Dagger-grave and other Cist Burials at Ashgrove, Methilhill, Fife', *Proceedings of the Royal Society of Antiquaries of Scotland* 97: 166–179.

Hill, J. & Richards, C. 2005. 'Structure 8: Monumentality at Barnhouse', *Dwelling among the monuments: the Neolithic village of Barnhouse, Maeshowe passage grave and surrounding monuments at Stenness, Orkney*. Oxford: Oxbow. 157–194.

Hodder, I. 1979. 'Economic and Social Stress and Material Culture Patterning', *American Antiquity* 44: 446–454.

Hosler, D. 1995. 'Sound, Colour and Meaning in the Metallurgy of Ancient Mexico', *World Archaeology* 27: 100–115.

Iriarte, J., Gillam, J. C. & Marozzi, O. 2007. 'Monumental burials and memorial feasting: an example from the southern Brazilian highlands', *Antiquity* 82: 947–961.

Jenkins, A. V. C. 1991. 'The Human Bone: Inhumations', in P. S. Bellamy, The Excavation of Fordington Farm Round Barrow. *Proceedings of the Dorset Natural History and Archaeological Society* 113. 119–121.

Johnston, D. A. 1997. 'Biggar Common, 1987–93: an early prehistoric funerary and domestic landscape in Clydesdale, South Lanarkshire', *Proceedings of the Society of Antiquaries of Scotland* 127: 185–253.

Jones, A. 2006. 'Animated Images: Images, Agency and Landscape in Kilmartin, Argyll, Scotland', *Journal of Material Culture*: 211–225.

Jones, A. 2007. 'Excavating Art: Recent Excavations at the Rock-Art Sites at Torbhlaren, near Kilmartin, Mid-Argyll, Scotland', *Past* 57: 1–3.

Jones, A., Cole, W. J. 2005. 'Organic Residue Analysis of Grooved Ware from Barnhouse', in C. Richards (ed.) *Dwelling among the monuments: the Neolithic village of Barnhouse, Maeshowe passage grave and surrounding monuments at Stenness, Orkney.* Oxford: Oxbow: 283–291.

Kahn, M. 1990. 'Stone-Faced Ancestors: The Spatial Anchoring of Myth in Wamira, Papua New Guinea', *Ethnology* 29: 51–66.

Keeley, L. 1997. *War Before Civilization: The Myth of the Peaceful Savage.* Oxford: Oxford University Press.

Keith, A. 1915. 'Presidential Address: The Bronze Age Invaders of Britain', *The Journal of the Royal Anthropological Institute of Great Britain & Ireland* 45: 12–22.

Kennedy. J. G. 1971. 'Ritual and Intergroup Murder: Comments on War, Primitive and Modern', in M. N. Walsh (ed.) *War and the Human Race.* London: Elsevier. 40–61.

Kolb, M. J. & Dixon, B. 2002. 'Landscapes of War: Rules and Conventions of Conflict in Ancient Hawai'i (And Elsewhere)', *American Antiquity* 67: 514–534.

Kramer, C. 1985. 'Ceramic Ethnoarchaeology', *Annual Review of Anthropology* 14: 77–102.

Lambert, P. M. 2002. 'The Archaeology of War: A North American Perspective', *Journal of Anthropological Research* 10: 207–241.

Last, J. 1998. 'Books of Life: Biography and Memory in a Bronze Age Barrow', *Oxford Journal of Archaeology* 17: 43–53.

Lawson, A. 1992. 'Stonehenge: creating a definitive account', *Antiquity* 66: 934–941.

Lawson, A. J. 1993. 'A late Neolithic Chalk Plaque from Butterfield Down, Wiltshire', *The Antiquaries Journal*: 183–185.

Leary, J. 2011. 'Making Sense of Silbury', *British Archaeology* 116: 39–43.

Lewis-Williams, J. D. 1987. 'A Dream of Eland: An Unexplored Component of San Shamanism and Rock Art', *World Archaeology* 19: 165–177.

Lewis-Williams, J. D. 1988. 'The Signs of All Times: Entopic Phenomena in Upper Palaeolithic Art', *Current Anthropology* 29: 201–245.

Lewis-Williams, J. D. 1996. 'Agency, art and altered consciousness: a motif in French (Quercy) Upper Palaeolithic art', *Antiquity* 71: 810–830.

Long, D. J., Milburn, P., Bunting, M. J. & Tipping, R. 1999. 'Black Henbane (*Hyoscyamus niger* L.) in the Scottish Neolithic: A Re-evaluation of Palynological Findings from Grooved Ware potter at Balfarg Riding School and Henge, Fife', *Journal of Archaeological Science* 26: 45–52.

Long, D. J., Tipping, R., Holden, T. G., Bunting, M. J. & Milburn, P. 2000. 'The use of henbane (*Hyoscyamus niger* L.) as a hallucinogen at Neolithic 'ritual' sites: a re-evaluation', *Antiquity* 74: 49–53.

Longworth, I. 1999. 'The Folkton Drums Unpicked', in R. Cleal & A. MacSween (eds) *Grooved Ware in Britain and Ireland (Neolithic Studies Group Seminar Papers 3)*. Oxford: Oxbow: 83–88.

Lynch, F., Aldhouse-Green, S. & Davies, J. L. 2000. *Prehistoric Wales*. Stroud: Sutton.

Macdonald, M. 2006. 'A note on the diameters of carved stone balls', *Proceedings of the Society of Antiquaries of Scotland* 136: 75–76.

Mackie, E. W. 1977. *Science and Society in Prehistoric Britain*. New York: St Martin's Press.

MacKie, E. W. 1997. 'Maeshowe and the winter solstice: ceremonial aspects of the Grooved Ware culture', *Antiquity* 71: 338–359.

Maclagan Wedderburn, L. M. 1970–71. 'A Short Cist Burial At Hatton Mill Farm, Friockheim, Angus', *Proceedings of the Society of Antiquaries of Scotland* 102: 82–86.

Mann, L. M. 1913–14. 'The Carved Stone Balls of Scotland: a New Theory as to their Use', *Proceedings of the Society of Antiquaries of Scotland* 48: 201–219.

Marshall, D. N. 1976–77. 'Carved stone balls', *Proceedings of the Society of Antiquaries of Scotland* 108: 40–72.

McCartan. S. 2004. 'Flaked Stone Assemblages', in W. O'Brien (ed) *Ross Island: Mining, Metal and Society in Early Ireland*. Galway: National University of Ireland Bronze Age Studies 6.

McKinley, J. 2011. 'Bare Bones: The "Amesbury Archer" and the "Boscombe Bowmen"', *Current Archaeology* 251: 12–19.

Megaw, J. V. S. 1960. 'Penny Whistles and Prehistory', *Antiquity* XXXIV: 6–13.

Mercer, R. 2006. 'By Other Means? The Development of Warfare in the British Isles 3000–500 B.C.' *Journal of Conflict Archaeology* 2: 119–152.

Merlin, M. D. 2003. 'Archaeological Evidence for the Tradition of Psychoactive Plant Use in the Old World', *Economic Botany* 57: 295–323.

Meyer, C., Brandt, G., Haak, W., Ganslmeier, R. A., Meller, H. & Alt, K. W. 2009. 'The Eulau eulogy: Bioarchaeological interpretation of lethal violence in Corded Ware multiple burials from Saxony-Anhalt, Germany', *Journal of Anthropological Archaeology* 28: 412–423.

Middleton, A., Young, J. R. & Ambers, J. 2004. 'The Folkton Drums: chalk or cheese?' *Antiquity* 78: Project Gallery.

Milner, G. R. 1999. 'Warfare in Prehistoric and Early Historic Eastern North America', *Journal of Archaeological Research* 7: 105–151.

Milner, G. R. 2005. 'Nineteenth-Century Arrow Wounds and Perceptions of Prehistoric Warfare', *American Antiquity* 70: 144–156.

Mitchell, D. 1984. 'Predatory Warfare, Social Status, and the North Pacific Slave Trade', *Ethnology* 23: 39–48.

Moffat, B. 1993. 'An assessment of residues on the Grooved Ware', in G. J. Barclay & C. J. Russell White (eds) Excavations in the ceremonial complex of the fourth to second millennium BC at Balfarg/Balbirnie, Glenrothes, Fife. *Proceedings of the Society of Antiquaries of Scotland* 123: 108–110.

Mohen, J-P. 1999. *Standing Stones: Stonhenge, Carnac and the World of the Megaliths*. London: Thames & Hudson.

Monks, S. J. 1997. 'Conflict and Competition in Spanish Prehistory: The Role of Warfare in Societal Development from the Late Fourth to Third Millennium BC', *Journal of Mediterranean Archaeology* 10: 3–32.

Montelius, O. 1908. *The Chronology of the British Bronze Age*, London: Society of Antiquaries.

Montgomery, J., Cooper, R. & Evans, J. 2007. 'Foragers, farmers or foreigners? An assessment of dietary strontium isotope variation in Middle Neolithic and Early Bronze Age East Yorkshire', in M. Larsson & M. Parker Pearson (eds) *From Stonehenge to the Baltic: Living with cultural diversity in the third millennium BC*. British Archaeological Reports (International Series) 1692: 65–77.

Morris, R. W. B. 1970–71. 'The Petroglyphs at Achnabreck, Argyll', *Proceedings of the Society of Antiquaries of Scotland*: 33–56.

Mount, C. 1994. 'Aspects of Ritual Deposition in the Late Neolithic and Beaker Periods at Newgrange, Co. Meath', *Proceedings of the Prehistoric Society* 60: 433–443.

Mukherjee, A. J., Berstan, R., Copley, M. S., Gibson, A. M., Evershed, R. P. 2007. 'Compound-specific stable carbon isotopic detection of pig product processing in British Late Neolithic pottery', *Antiquity* 81: 743–754.

Mukherjee, A. J., Gibson, A. M., Evershed, R. P. 2008. 'Trends in pig product processing at British Neolithic Grooved Ware sites traced through organic residues in potsherds', *Journal of Archaeological Science* 35: 2059–2073.

Mullin, D. 2008. 'Is there a British Chalcolithic? People, Place and Polity in the Later Third Millenium BC', *Past* 60: 6–7.

Murphy, E. & Simpson, D. 2003. 'Neolithic Norton: a review of the evidence', in I. Armit, E. Murphy, E. Nelis & D. Simpson (eds) *Neolithic Settlement in Ireland and Western Britain*. Oxford: Oxbow.

Nash, P. 2006. 'Light at the end of the tunnel: the way megalithic art was viewed and experienced', *Documenta Praehistorica* XXXIII: 209–227.

Needham, S. P. 1988. 'Selective deposition in the British Early Bronze Age', *World Archaeology* 20: 229–248.

Needham, S. 1999. 'Wider Contacts: Early Metalworking and its implications', in A. Barclay & C. Halpin (eds) *Excavations at Barrow Hills, Radley,*

Oxfordshire. Volume 1: The Neolithic and Bronze Age Monument Complex. Oxford: Oxford Archaeological Unit: 327–328

Needham, S. 2001. 'Prehistoric Artefacts 1. Braithwaite, South Yorkshire: Early Bronze Age gold crescent'. Treasure Annual Report. http://finds.org.uk/documents/treasurereports/2001.pdf

Needham, S. 2005. 'Transforming Beaker Culture in North-West Europe; Processes of Fusion and Fission', *Proceedings of the Prehistoric Society* 71: 171–217.

Needham, S. 2007. 'Isotopic Aliens: Beaker movement and cultural transmissions', in M. Larsson & M. Parker Pearson (eds) *From Stonehenge to the Baltic: Living with cultural diversity in the third millennium BC*. Oxford: British Archaeological Reports (International Series) 1692: 41–47.

Needham, S., Pitts, M., Heyd, V., Parker Pearson, M., Jay, M., Montgomery, J. & Sheridan, S. 2008. 'In the Copper Age', *British Archaeology* 101: 19–27.

Nicklin, K. 1971. 'Stabilty and Innovation in Pottery Manufacture', *World Archaeology* 3: 13–48.

Nicklin, K. 1979. 'The Location of Pottery Manufcature', *Man* 14: 436–458.

Northover, P. 1999. 'Analysis of Early Bronze Age Metalwork from Barrow Hills', in A. Barclay & C. Halpin (eds) *Excavations at Barrow Hills, Radley, Oxfordshire. Volume 1: The Neolithic and Bronze Age Monument Complex*. Oxford: Oxford Archaeological Unit: 192–195.

O'Brien, W. 1990. 'Prehistoric Copper Mining in South-West Ireland: The Mount Gabriel-Type Mines', *Proceedings of the Prehistoric Society* 56: 269–290.

O'Brien, W. 1996. *Bronze Age Copper Mining in Britain and Ireland*. Princes Risborough: Shire.

O'Brien, W. 2004. *Ross Island: Mining, Metal and Society in Early Ireland*. Galway: National University of Ireland Department of Archaeology Bronze Age Studies 6.

O'Flaherty, R. 1998. 'The Early Bronze age Halberd: A History of Research and a Brief Guide to the Sources', *The Journal of the Royal Society of Antiquaries of Ireland* 128: 74–94.

O'Flaherty, R. 2007. 'A weapon of choice – experiments with a replica Irish Early Bronze Age halberd', *Antiquity* 312: 423–434.

Osgood, R., Monks, S. with Toms, J. 2000. *Bronze Age Warfare*. Stroud: Sutton.

Ottaway, B. S. 2001. 'Innovation, Production and Specialization in Early Prehistoric Copper Metallurgy', *European Journal of Archaeology* 4: 87–112.

Parker Pearson, M. 2005. *Bronze Age Britain*. London: B. T. Batsford/English Heritage.

Parker Pearson, M. 2007. 'The Stonehenge Riverside Project: excavations at the east entrance to Durrington Walls', in M. Larsson & M. Parker Pearson (eds) *From Stonehenge to the Baltic: Living with cultural diversity in the third millennium BC*. British Archaeological Reports (International Series) 1692: 125–144.

Parker Pearson, M., Chamberlain, C., Jay, M., Marshall, P., Pollard, J., Richards, C., Thomas, J., Tilley, C. & Welham, K. 2009. 'Who was buried at Stonehenge?' *Antiquity* 83: 23–39.

Parker Pearson, M., Cleal, R., Marshall, P., Needham, S., Pollard, J., Richards, C., Ruggles, C., Sheridan, A., Thomas, J., Tilley, C., Welham, K., Chamberlain, A., Chenery, C., Evans, J., Knüsel, C., Linford, N., Martin, L., Montgomery, J., Payne, A. & Richards. M. 2007. 'The age of Stonehenge', *Antiquity* 81: 617–639.

Parker Pearson, M., Pollard, J., Richards, C., Thomas, J., Tilley, C., Welham, K. & Albarella, U. 2006. 'Materializing Stonehenge: The Stonehenge Riverside Project and New Discoveries', *Journal of Material Culture* 11: 227–261.

Parker Pearson, M. & Ramilisonina. 1998. 'Stonehenge for the ancestors: the stones pass on the message', *Antiquity* 72: 308–326.

Parker Pearson, M. & Ramilisonina. 1998. 'Stonehenge for the ancestors: part two', *Antiquity* 72: 855–856.

Peate, I. C. 1925a. 'Arrow-heads from Bugeilyn', *Archaeologia Cambrensis* LXXX: 196–202.

Peate, I. C. 1925b. 'Arrow-heads from Bugeilyn', *Archaeologia Cambrensis* LXXX: 415–416.

Peate, I. C. 1928. 'More Arrowheads from Bugeilyn', Archaeologia Cambrensis LXXXIII: 344–345.

Piggott, S. 1941. 'The Sources of Geoffrey of Monmouth. II. The Stonehenge Story', *Antiquity* XV: 305–319.

Piggott, S. 1954. *The Neolithic Cultures of the British Isles: A Study of the Stone-using Agricultural Communities of Britain in the Second Millennium B.C.* Cambridge: Cambridge University Press.

Piggott, S. 1971. 'Beaker bows: a suggestion', *Proceedings of the Prehistoric Society* 37: 80–94

Piggott, S. 1971–72 'Excavation of the Dalladies long barrow, Fettercairn, Kincardineshire', *Proceedings of the Society of Antiquaries of Scotland* 104: 23–47.

Pitts, M. 2001. *Hengeworld*. London. Arrow.

Pitts, M. 2003. 'Don't knock the ancestors', *Antiquity* 77: 172–178.

Pitts, M. 2005. 'Unique art in conservation dilemma', *British Archaeology* 81: 6.

Pitts, M. 2008. 'Was Missing Body a Dutchman in Scotland?', *British Archaeology* 99: 6.

Pitts, M. 2009. 'A year at Stonehenge', *Antiquity* 83: 184–194.

Pitts, M. & Whittle, A. 1992. 'The development and date of Avebury', *Proceedings of the Prehistoric Society* 58: 203–212.

Plog, S. 1983, 'Analysis of Style in Artifacts', *Annual Review of Anthropology* 12: 125–142.

Pollard. J. 1992. 'The Sanctuary, Overton Hill, Wiltshire: a re-examination', *Proceedings of the Prehistoric Society* 58: 213–226.

Pollard, J. 2001. 'The aesthetics of depositional practice', *World Archaeology* 33: 315–333.

Price, B. 2007. 'Journeying into different realms: travel, pilgrimage and rites of passage at Graig Lwyd', in V. Cummings & R. Johnston (eds) *Prehistoric Journeys*. Oxford: Oxbow.

Price, T. D., Grupe, G. & Schröter, P. 1998. 'Migration in the Bell Beaker period of Central Europe', *Antiquity* 72: 405–411.

Price, T. D., Knipper, C, Grupe, G. & Smrcka, V. 2004. 'Strontium Isotopes and Prehsitoric Human Migration: The Bell Beaker Period in Central Europe', *European Journal of Archaeology* 7: 9–40.

Prieto-Martínez, M. P. 2008. 'Bell Beaker Communities in Thy: The First Bronze Age Society in Denmark', *Norwegian Archaeological Review* 41. 115–158.

Pryor, F. 2002. *Seahenge: A Quest for Life and Death in Bronze Age Britain*. London: Harper Collins.

Pryor, F. 2003. *Britain BC: Life in Britain and Ireland before the Romans*. London: Harper Collins.

Redfern, N. & Vyner, B. 2009: 'Fylingdales Moor: a lost landscape rises from the ashes', *Current Archaeology* 226: 20–27.

Reedy-Maschner, H. D. G. & Reedy-Maschner, K. L. 1998. 'Raid, Retreat, Defend (Repeat): The Archaeology and Ethnohistory of Warfare on the North Pacific Rim', *Journal of Anthropological Archaeology* 17: 19–51.

Renfrew, C. 1969. 'Trade and Culture Process in European Prehsitory', *Current Anthropology* 10: 151–169.

Renfrew, C. 1973. *Before Civilization: The Radiocarbon Revolution and Prehistoric Europe*. London: Pimlico.

Renfrew, C. 1978. 'Varna and the social context of early metallurgy', *Antiquity* LII: 199–203

Richards, C. 1996. 'Henges and Water: Towards an Elemental Understanding of Monumentality and Landscape in Late Neolithic Britain', *Journal of Material Culture* 1: 313–336.

Richards, C. 1996. 'Monuments as landscape: creating the centre of the world in late Neolithic Orkney', *World Archaeology* 28: 190–208.

Richards, C. & Thomas, J. 1984. 'Ritual activity and structured deposition in Later Neolithic Wessex', in R. Bradley & J. Gardiner (eds) *Neolithic Studies: A Review of Some Current Research*, British Archaeological Reports (British Series) 133: 189–218.

Ripoll, S., Muñoz, F., Bahn, P. & Pettit, P. 2004. 'Palaeolithic cave engravings at Creswell Crags, England', *Proceedings of the Prehistoric Society* 70: 93–105.

Ritchie, A. 1995. *Prehistoric Orkney*. London: B. T. Batsford.

Ritchie, J. N. G. & Crawford, J. 1977–78. 'Recent work on Coll and Skye: (i) Excavations at Sorisdale and Killunaig, Coll', *Proceedings of the Royal Society of Antiquaries of Scotland* 109: 75–84.

Roberts, B. 2008. 'Creating traditions and shaping technologies: understanding the earliest metal objects and metal production in Western Europe', *World Archaeology* 40: 354–372.

Roberts, B. W., Thornton., C. P. & Piggot, V. C. 2009. 'Development of Metallurgy in Eurasia', *Antiquity* 83: 1012–1022.

Roe, F. E. S. 1966. 'The Battle-Axe Series in Britain', *Proceedings of the Prehistoric Society* XXXII: 199–245

Ruggles, C. 1999. *Astronomy in Prehistoric Britain and Ireland*. London/New Haven: Yale University Press.

Russel, A. D. 1990. 'Two Beaker burials from Chilbolton, Hampshire', *Proceedings of the Prehistoric Society* 56: 153–172.

Sackett, J. R. 1977. 'The Meaning of Style in Archaeology: A General Model', *American Antiquity* 42: 369–380.

Sarauw, T. 2008. 'Danish Bell Beaker Pottery and Flint Daggers – the Display of Social Indenties', *European Journal of Archaeology* 11: 23–47.

Saville, A. 1994. 'A decorated Skaill knife from Skara Brae. Orkney', *Proceedings of the Antiquaries of Scotland* 124: 103–111.

Schuhmacher, T. X. 2002. 'Some Remarks on the Origin and Chronology of Halberds in Europe', *Oxford Journal of Archaeology* 21: 263–288.

Scarre, C. 1998. *Exploring Prehistoric Europe*. Oxford: Oxford University Press.

Scott. B. G. 1977. 'Drink or Drugs? Comments on the "Beaker Cult Package", *Irish Archaeological Research Forum* 4: 29–34.

Selkirk. A. 2008. 'Stonehenge revealed: How much of the monument is Roman?' *Current Archaeology* 219: 12–17.

Sharpe. K., Barnett, T., Rushton, S. & Bryan, P. 2008. *The Prehistoric Rock Art of England: Recording, managing and enjoying our carved heritage*. English Heritage/ Northumberland County Council. http://archaeologydataservice.ac.uk/era

Shennan, S. J. 1987. 'Trends in the Study of Later European Prehistory', *Annual Review of Anthropology* 16: 365–382.

Shepherd, I. A. G. 2009. 'The V-bored buttons of Great Britain & Ireland', *Proceedings of the Prehistoric Society* 75: 335–369.

Shepherd, I. A. G. & Tuckwell, A. N. 1976–77. 'Traces of beaker-period cultivation at Rosinish, Benbecula', *Proceedings of the Society of Antiquaries of Scotland*: 108–113.

Sheridan, A. 1997. 'Pottery', in D. A. Johnston (ed.) 'Biggar Common, 1987–93: an early prehistoric funerary and domestic landscape in Clydesdale, South Lanarkshire', *Proceedings of the Society of Antiquaries of Scotland* 127: 202–223.

Sheridan, A. 2007. 'Scottish Beaker dates: the good, the bad and the ugly', in M. Larsson & M. Parker Pearson (eds) *From Stonehenge to the Baltic: Living with cultural diversity in the third millennium BC*. Oxford: British Archaeological Reports (International Series) 1692: 91–125.

Sheridan, A. 2008a. *Towards a fuller, more nuanced narrative of Chalcolithic and Early Bronze Britain 2500–1500 BC*. London: British Museum Bronze Age Review 1: 57–78.

Sheridan, J. A. 2008b. 'Upper Largie and Dutch-Scottish connections during the Beaker period', in H. Fokkens, B. J. Coles, A. L. van Gijn, J. P. Kleijne,

H. H. Ponjeee & C. G. Slappendel (eds) *Between Foraging and Farming: an Extended Broad Spectrum of Papers Presented to Leendert Louwe Kooijmans.* Leiden: Analects Praehistorica Leidensia 40: 247–260.

Sherratt, A. 1986. 'The Radley "Earrings" Revised', *Oxford Journal of Archaeology* 5: 61–66.

Sherratt, A. 1987. 'Cups That Cheered', in W. H. Waldren & R. C. Kennard (eds) *Bell Beakers of the Western Mediterranean.* British Archaeological Reports (International Series) 331(i): 81–114.

Sherratt, A. 1995. 'Alcohol and its Alternatives: Symbol and substance in pre-industrial cultures', in J. Goodman, P. E. Lovejoy & A. Sherrat (eds) *Consuming Habits: Drugs in History and Anthropology.* London: Routledge. 11–46.

Sherratt, A. 1997. 'The Transformation of Early Agrarian Europe: The Later Neolithic and Copper Ages 4500–2500 BC', in B. Cunliffe (ed.) *Prehistoric Europe: An Illustrated History.* Oxford: Oxford University Press.

Skak-Nielsen, N. V. 2008. 'Flint and metal daggers in Scandinavia and other parts of Europe. A re-interpretation of their function in the Late Neolithic and Early Copper and Bronze Age', *Antiquity* 83: 349–358.

Smith, J. A. 1874–76. 'Notes of Small Ornamented Stone Balls found in Different Parts of Scotland', *Proceedings of the Society of Antiquaries of Scotland* 11: 29–62.

Souden, D. 1997. *Stonehenge: Mysteries of the Stones and Landscape.* London: Collins & Brown.

Starling, N. J. 1985. 'Social change in the Later Neolithic of Central Europe', *Antiquity* LIX: 30–38.

Sterner, J. 1989. 'Who is signalling whom? Ceramic style, ethnicity and taphonomy among the Sirak Bulahay', *Antiquity* 63: 451–459.

Stevenson, R. B. K. 1956–57. 'A Bone Ring from a Beaker Burial at Mainsriddle, Kirkcudbrightshire', *Proceedings of the Society of Antiquaries of Scotland* 90: 229–231.

Suddaby, I. & Sheridan, S. 2006. 'A pit containing an undecorated Beaker and associated artefacts from Beechwood Park, Raigmore, Inverness', *Proceedings of the Society of Antiquaries of Scotland* 136: 77–89.

Sundstrom, L. 1996. 'Mirror of heaven: cross-cultural transference of the sacred geography of the Black Hills', *World Archaeology* 28: 177–189.

Taçon, P. S. C., 1991. 'The power of stone: symbolic aspects of stone use and tool development in western Arnhem Land, Australia', *Antiquity* 65: 192–207.

Taylor, J. J. 1970. 'Lunulae Reconsidered', *Proceedings of the Prehistoric Society* XXXVI: 38–81

Taylor, J. J. 1985. 'Gold and Silver (The Importance of Craftsmen)', in D. V. Clarke, T. G. Cowie & A. Foxon (eds) *Symbols of Power at the Time of Stonehenge.* Edinburgh: Her Majesty's Stationery Office: 182–192.

Taylor, J. J. 1994. 'The First Golden Age of Europe was in Britain and Ireland (Circa 2400–1400 BC)', *Ulster Journal of Archaeology* 57: 37–60.

Thomas, J. 1987. 'Relations of Production and Social Change in the Neolithic of North-West Europe', *Man* 22: 405–430.

Thomas, J. 1999. *Understanding the Neolithic*. Oxon: Routledge.

Thomas, J. 2007. 'The internal features at Durrington Walls: investigations in the Southern Circle and Western Enclosures', in M. Larsson & M. Parker Pearson (eds) *From Stonehenge to the Baltic: Living with cultural diversity in the third millennium BC*. British Archaeological Reports (International Series) 1692: 145–158.

Thomas, J. 2010. 'The Return of the Rinyo-Clacton Folk? The Cultural Significance of the Grooved Ware Complex in Later Neolithic Britain', *Cambridge Archaeological Journal* 20: 1–15.

Thompson, F. C. 1958. 'The Early Metallurgy of Copper and Bronze: A Report to the Ancient Mining and Metallurgy Committee of the Royal Anthropological Institute', *Man* 1: 1–7

Thorpe, N. 2000. 'Origins of War: Mesolithic Conflict in Europe', *British Archaeology* 52: 9–13.

Thorpe, N. 2006. 'Fighting and Feuding in Neolithic and Bronze Age Britain and Ireland', in T. Otto, H. Thrane & H. Vandkilde (eds) *Warfare and Society: Archaeological and Social Anthropological Perspectives*. Aarhus: Aarhus University Press. 141–166.

Thorpe, I. J. & Richards, C. 1984. 'The Decline of Ritual Authority and the Introduction of Beakers into Britain', in R. Bradley & J. Gardiner (eds) Neolithic Studies: *A Review of Some Current Research*. British Archaeological Reports (British Series): 67–84.

Thorpe, R. S. & Williams-Thorpe, O. 1991. 'The myth of long-distance megalith transport', *Antiquity* 65: 64–73.

Timberlake, S. 2003. *Excavations on Copa Hill, Cwmystwyth (1986–1999): An Early Bronze Age copper mine within the uplands of Central Wales*. Oxford: British Archaeological Reports 348.

Timberlake, S., Gwilt, A. & Davis, M. 2004. 'A Copper Age/early Bronze Age gold disc from Banc Tynddol (Penguelan, Cymystwyth Mines, Ceridigion)', *Antiquity* 78: Project Gallery.

Timberlake, S. 2009. 'Copper mining and metal production at the beginning of the British Bronze Age', in P. Clark (ed.) *Bronze age Connections: Cultural Contacts in Prehistoric Europe*. Oxford: Oxbow: 94–122.

Timberlake, S. & Prag, A. J. N. W. 2005. *The Archaeology of Alderley Edge: Survey, excavation and experiment in an ancient mining landscape*. Oxford: British Archaeological Reports (British Series) 396.

Tobert, N. 1984. 'Ethno-Archaeology of Pottery Firing in Darfur, Sudan: Implications for Ceramic Technology Studies', *Oxford Journal of Archaeology* 3: 141–156.

Todd, T. N. 2006. 'The aerodynamics of carved stone balls', *Proceedings of the Society of Antiquaries of Scotland* 136: 61–74.

Topping, P. 2003. *Grime's Graves*. London. English Heritage.

Topping, P. 2005. 'Shaft 27 Revisited: an Ethnography of Neolithic Flint Extraction', in P. Topping & M. Lynott (eds) *The Cultural Landscape of Prehistoric Mines*. Oxford: Oxbow: 63–93.

Turek, J. 2004. 'Craft Symbolism in the Bell Beaker burial customs: resources, production and social structure at the end of the Eneolithic period', in M. Besse & J. Desideri (eds) *Graves and Funerary Rituals during the Late Neolithic and Early Bronze Age in Europe (2700–2000 BC)*. Oxford: British Archaeological Reports (International Series) 1284: 147–156.

Turner, V. 1998. *Ancient Shetland*. London: B. T. Batsford/Historic Scotland.

Treherne, P. 1995. 'The Warrior's Beauty: The Masculine and Self-Identity in Bronze-Age Europe', *Journal of European Archaeology* 3: 105–144.

Vacher, F. de M. 1969. 'Two incised Chalk Plaques from near Stonehenge Bottom', *Antiquity* 43: 310–311.

Vankilde, H. 2006. 'Warriors and Warrior Institutions in Copper Age Europe' in T. Otto, H. Thrane & H. Vankilde (eds) *Warfare and Society: Archaeological and Social Anthropological Perspectives*. Aarhus: Aarhus University Press: 393–422.

Vander Linden, M. 2006. 'For Whom the Bell Tolls: Social Hierarchy vs Social Integration in the Bell Beaker Culture of Southern France', *Cambridge Archaeological Journal* 16: 317–332.

Vander Linden, M. 2007. 'For equalities are plural: reassessing the social in Europe during the third millennium BC', *World Archaeology* 39: 177–193.

Vander Linden, M. 2007. 'What linked the Bell Beakers in third millennium BC Europe?' *Antiquity* 81: 343–352.

Varndell, G. 1999. 'An Engraved Chalk Plaque from Hanging Cliff, Kilham', *Journal of Oxford Archaeology* 18: 351–355.

Waddell, J. 2000. *The Prehistoric Archaeology of Ireland*. Wicklow: Wordwell.

Waddington, C. 1998. 'Cup and Ring marks in Context', *Cambridge Archaeological Journal* 8: 29–54.

Watson, A. 2001. 'Composing Avebury', *World Archaeology* 33: 296–314.

Watkins, T. & Shepherd, I. A. G. 1978–80. 'A Beaker Burial at Newmill, near Bankfoot, Perthshire', *Proceedings of the Society of Antiquaries of Scotland* 110: 32–43.

Wessex Archaeology 2009. 'A ritual landscape at Boscombe Down'. http://www.wessexarch.co.uk/projects/wiltshire/boscombe/ritual-landscape-boscombe-down

Whitley, D. S. 1992. 'Shamanism and Rock Art in Far Western North America', *Cambridge Archaeological Journal* 2: 89–113.

Whitley, D. S., Loubser, J. H. N. & Hann, D. 2004. 'Friends in low places: rock art and landscape on the Modoc Plateau' in C. Chippindale & G. Nash (eds) *Pictures in Place: The Figured Landscapes of Rock-Art*. Cambridge: Cambridge University Press: 217–238.

Whitley, J. W. 2002. 'Too many ancestors', *Antiquity* 291: 199–126.

Whitley, J. W. 2003. 'Response to Mike Pitt's "Don't Knock the Ancestors"', *Antiquity* 296: 401.

Whittle, A. 1991. 'A late Neolithic complex at West Kennet, Wiltshire, England', *Antiquity*: 256–262.

Whittle, A. 1996. *Europe in the Neolithic: The Creation of New Worlds.* Cambridge: Cambridge University Press.

Whittle, A. 1997. *Sacred Mound Holy Rings. Silbury Hill and the West Kennet palisade enclosures: a Later Neolithic complex in north Wiltshire.* Oxford: Oxbow.

Whittle, A. 1998. 'People and the diverse past: two comments on Stonehenge for the ancestors', *Antiquity* 72: 852–854.

Whittle, A., Keith-Lucas, M., Milles, A., Noddle, B., Rees, S. & Romans, R. C. 1986. *Scord of Brouster: An Early Agricultural Settlement on Shetland.* Oxford: Oxford University Committee for Archaeology Monograph No. 9.

Van Wijngaarden-Bakker, L. 2004. 'The Animal Remains', in W. O'Brien (ed.) *Ross Ireland: Mining, Metal and Society in Early Ireland.* Galway: National University of Ireland Bronze Age Studies 6: 367–385.

Williams-Thorpe, O., Jenkins, D.G., Jenkins, J. & Watson, J. S. 1995. 'Chlorine-36 dating and the bluestones of Stonehenge', *Antiquity* 69: 1019–1020.

Williams-Thorpe, O., Jones, M. C., Potts, P. J. & Webb, P. C. 2006. 'Preseli Dolerite Bluestones: Axe-Heads, Stonehenge Monoliths, and Outcrop Sources', *Oxford Journal of Archaeology* 25: 29–46.

Wise, K. 2002. 'High-mountain Inca Sacrifices', in P. Bahn (ed.) *Written in Bones: How Human Remains Unlock the Secrets of the Dead.* Devon: David & Charles: 119–123.

Woodward, A. 2002. 'Beads and Beakers: heirlooms and relics in the British Early Bronze Age', *Antiquity* 76: 1040–1047.

Woodward, A. 2008. *Bronze Age pottery and settlements in southern England.* British Museum Bronze Age Review 1: 79–96

Young, A. 2008. 'Knobs, Spirals, Fire and Platonic Solids', *British Archaeology* 99: 43–45.

Index

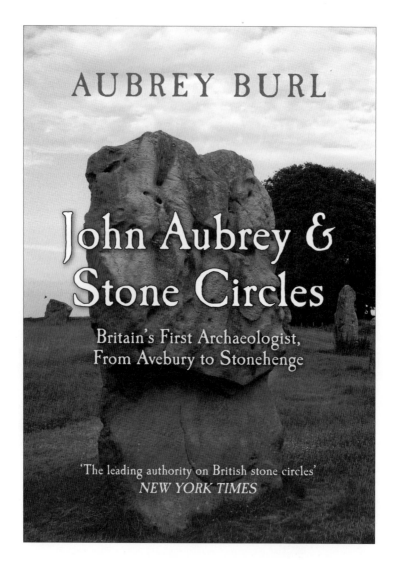